NOW WHERE WAS I?

NOW WHERE WAS I?
A Sketchbook Memoir

by Steven B. Reddy

© 2014 by Steven B. Reddy

All rights reserved. No part of this book may be reproduced in any form whatsoever without permission in writing from the author, except by a reviewer who may quote brief passages in review.

ISBN-13: 978-0-615-92152-5

Library of Congress Control Number: 2013921634

Printed in the USA

stevenreddy.com

To order additional books visit:
etsy.com/shop/StevenReddy

For information or bulk orders, email:
BooShackBooks@gmail.com

Cover drawing:
50th St. Deli Market, *2013*
Watercolor, 11" x 18"

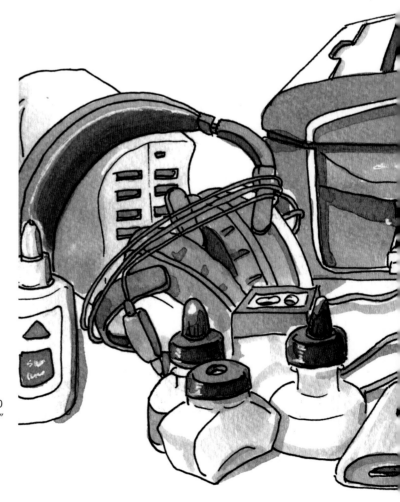

Desktop Clutter, 2010
Ink wash, 7" x 12"

For Donna

Singapore Elevator, 2011
Watercolor, 12" x 8.5"

CONTENTS

Acknowledgements	9
Introduction	11
A Place For My Stuff	13
El Golfo	22
Kalen	30
Seattle	40
Just Looking	57
Long Beach	77
Downsizing	86
Jingdezhen	96
Urban Sketching	132
Bangkok	160
Drawing People	164
Singapore	188
Origins	192
Acapulco	220
Oil Painting	228
Sidney	240
Teaching	244
Home Is Where The Art Is	254
Crowdsourcing	282
Index	290

Connecticut Junk Shop, 2013
Watercolor, 8.5" x 12"

ACKNOWLEDGMENTS

I want to thank artists Gabriel Campanario and Danny Gregory for their personal encouragement and tireless efforts to foster a world-wide community of sketchers.

It was a privilege to meet and draw with the sketchers in China, Bangkok and Singapore. They were, without exception, welcoming and gracious hosts. I want to thank especially Tia Boon Sim, Asnee Tansa, Patrick Ng, Ali Sajid and Tony Chua for their time and support.

Thanks to Jackie Helfgott for her friendship, provocative questions, and patience with my circular answers.

I will always be grateful to the multi-talented Dana Williams for showing me his private sketchbook journals and charming me into a lifelong addiction of recording the daily minutiae that comprise my life.

Carol Benge went through the text in an early draft, catching all my typos and ungood grammar. Errors that remain I added afterwards with my constant, sleep-deprived tinkering.

Big thanks to the many supporters who helped spread the word or contributed directly to the Kickstarter campaign that made printing this book possible. Especially: Roy Forbes, Rich Goodnight, Robin Fuchs, Florence and Edward Plonski, Margaret Bolger, Darold Anderson, Brad Mohr, Kamila Kanczugoiwski, and Christine Legere.

My students and their families have had my back for fifteen years. I woke up every day eager to get to the classroom. My years teaching at Lawton Elementary have been an adventure and a pleasure.

Finally, my biggest thank-you goes to my most encouraging fan, my mom, Karen Reddy.

INTRODUCTION

I prefer drawing to talking. Drawing is faster, and leaves less room for lies.

    -Le Corbusier

This book was compiled from over fifty sketchbooks filled between 1979 and 2013. Some of the older pages were done very quickly, in bed perhaps, the way one might read for a bit before turning out the light. Since 2009, with few exceptions, all of the drawings were done on location, following the Urban Sketchers' manifesto to "draw directly from observation."

Many of the sketches were completed while waiting for something else to happen: sitting in a car, during a lunch break, getting an oil change, or in the dentist chair waiting for the anesthetic to take effect. To keep this book a manageable length, I had to leave out many drawings that I like, including some that are unfinished, maybe too personal to share, or to protect the privacy of others.

To select the images for this book, I began with the first journal, from when I was 15, and chose drawings that still speak to me, either individually, or after considering how they would fit into the book as a whole. Although many of the drawings, especially the older ones, were not intended for public consumption, there's a lot of accumulated time and effort in the sketchbooks so I'm grateful for this opportunity to pull them off the dusty shelves and give them some exposure.

This is, primarily, a book of illustrations. While laying out the pages of *Now Where Was I?*, I referred to art books that have remained favorites of mine for decades. Lincoln Kirstein's *Paul Cadmus* (Chameleon Books, 1996) has a clean design and simple layout that doesn't distract from the artwork. *Hipgnosis: Walk Away René* (Dragon's World, 1978) tells the story of the British design firm responsible for many of the most popular album covers of the 1970s. Each short chapter in that book (and mine) is organized around a theme which helps make "reading" the book a primarily visual experience, with the text secondary. I've owned and studied that book for many years but only recently read the text from cover to cover. If my book holds its own with no-one reading the text, that's okay by me. My sketchbooks, after all, are almost text-free.

When I post my work on-line, I'm often asked what kind of pen I use, the dimensions of the drawing, what kind of paper, etc., so I've included technical information in the captions, along with anything unique or interesting about making certain drawings. I've also included several longer passages where I go into some detail about my working methods and materials for anyone interested in that sort of thing.

I want to share my story. My son has been hearing about my experiences since he was a small kid and often tells me, "Dad, you have to write this stuff down. You gotta make a book." I briefly considered letting the sketches speak for themselves and to stay out of their way. There's something pure about looking through someone's sketchbook uninterrupted, without their subjective clarifications and apologies. Chris Ware's *Acme Novelty Datebook* (Drawn and Quarterly, 2003) is an example of the courage it takes to publish work that was not intended for an audience of strangers—work that is candid and sometimes embarrassing for the artist (and the viewer). For this volume, I've limited my anecdotes, as much as possible, to those that relate to the drawings.

A final note on the book's structure: every other chapter is based on a different location where I have lived or spent considerable time drawing. These chapters are in chronological order. Between each location chapter is a digression that delves into a tangential topic. For example, the chapter called *Origins*, as you might assume, explores my early days as an obsessive chronicler. To keep the chapters thematically consistent, sometimes biographical details emerge out of order. This is, after all, how we recall our lives: something triggers a memory or a tangent leads us somewhere unintended. I've tried to keep my mental wandering to a minimum.

So there you have it. Read only the chapters that interest you. Read from the back to the front. Or don't read any of it— feel free to just look at the pictures.

Steven Reddy

A PLACE FOR MY STUFF

A house is just a pile of stuff with a cover on it. You can see that when you're taking off in an airplane. You look down, you see everybody's got a little pile of stuff. That's what your house is, a place to keep your stuff while you go out and get ... more stuff! Sometimes you gotta move, gotta get a bigger house. Why? No room for your stuff anymore.

    -George Carlin

I don't know what to say when people ask me where I'm from. I've lived in over fifty houses and apartments. I was born in Omaha, Nebraska but before I was three my Mom, Dad and little brother moved to Tacoma, Washington. I vaguely recall a house overlooking water. My mother hanging laundry outside to dry. Fireworks. Daring myself to ride my red trike through an ant nest. In the middle of second grade my parents divorced and my mom rented a tiny duplex in Lakewood. She soon remarried and my step-dad moved us to Puyallup. My new elementary school became overcrowded so the fourth graders were moved to a nearby junior high. When Sunrise Elementary was built a few miles away that's where I went for sixth grade. A few months after settling into Ballou Junior High we moved again. We lived for three months on Kodiak Island, Alaska. And so on. By the time I graduated high school in Anchorage, I had changed schools thirteen times.

    When I left home for college, change was a way of life. I attended five colleges before getting my Bachelor of Fine Arts from the University of Oregon. I lived in my car for a short time, selling my plasma twice a week to buy granola and gasoline until they said I was too anemic to donate. I propped a board against the steering wheel to do my homework and showered in the university gym. When an ad agency internship turned into a job I rented a room.

    Three more colleges and I had a teaching certificate. Along the way I attended bartending school, completed a Community Access Television course, received a certificate in Teaching English as a Foreign Language and took several random classes at Community Colleges—mostly courses in acting, art and music. And lots of classes in ballroom dancing. Go figure.

    Maybe my transient lifestyle stunted my social maturity. People and places were temporary, so investing myself didn't seem prudent. I was emotionally sloppy since the end was always near and inevitable. Forming and maintaining long-term relationships is still hard work. My love life is an abandoned game of 52 Card Pick-Up.

    A consistent thread through this patchwork quilt of a history has been drawing. Through all the packing up and changing addresses, new schools and moving cities, the new relationships and the break-ups, I've managed to keep intact my dozens and dozens of sketchbooks. They fill the bookcase behind me, within arm's reach of this desk. As a matter of fact, everything I own, except for my bicycle, which is in the back of my car outside, is in this studio. I can swivel around in my rolling chair and see all my stuff. Sketchbooks, mostly. If I could I'd pack it all into this one book, "a pile of stuff with a cover on it."

Sarah's House, 2013
Watercolor, 12" x 9"

The parent of a former student commissioned me to draw her sister's home. The front of the house faces north so when I arrived around noon, the most interesting part of the house was shaded. I waited all day for the sun to hit the porch so I'd have some nice shadows to paint. The white balusters (the twenty or so vertical posts along the porch) were all down and stored in the garage. Sarah brought one out for me so I could see the style. I posed one in several places along the rail to see how the light would hit them, then I faked it. I was tempted to draw the missing finial but I liked the asymmetry and drew it the way I saw it.

Independence Day, 2012
Watercolor, 8.5" x 12"

My Humble Abode, 2010
Watercolor, 8.5" x 11"

I lived in these tiny apartments off and on for several years. I left to move in with a girlfriend and then moved back. I owned a house for five years and came back again. The manager, William, let me paint the walls odd colors and never asked for a deposit.

Out My Window, 2012
Watercolor, 3.5" x 11"

Living in a Box, *2013*
Watercolor, 9" x 12"

The eight houses on pages 16-19 are located in the Magnolia neighborhood of Seattle. I chose houses that caught my eye because they were unusual or were easy to see from the street. I was drawn to density of detail: bricks, stairs, shrubbery. Some were chosen simply because they looked fun to draw.

She's a Brick House, *2013*
Watercolor, 8.5" x 12"

Up On the Hill, *2013*
Watercolor, 9" x 12"

A Man's Home is His Castle, *2013*
Watercolor, 8.5" x 12"

3212, 2013
Watercolor, 9" x 12"

I hung these eight drawings in a coffee shop in the heart of the Magnolia neighborhood. Several of the home-owners came in for coffee and recognized their houses on display and bought them. Never underestimate the pride of home-ownership.

Aja, 2013
Watercolor, 9" x 12"

In the Pink, 2013
Watercolor, 9" x 12"

Lego House, 2013
Watercolor, 9" x 12"

A Place For My Stuff

House On Greenlake, 2013
(Drawing the contours)

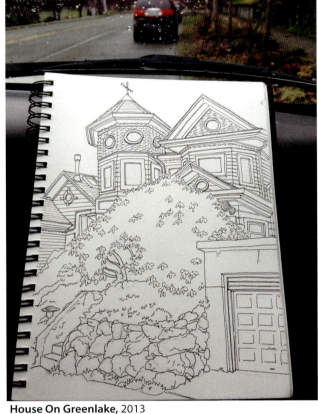

House On Greenlake, 2013
(Adding details)

House On Greenlake, 2013
(Ink wash grisaille)

House On Greenlake, 2013
(Completed grisaille)

House On Greenlake, 2013
Watercolor, 12" x 8.5"

Club House, 2010
Watercolor, 8.5" x 12"

EL GOLFO

Own only what you can always carry with you: know languages, know countries, know people. Let your memory be your travel bag.

  -Aleksandr Solzhenitsyn

My parents live in Mexico now, in a remote fishing village on the Sea of Cortez. Tired of the cold winters in Alaska and the gloomy skies of the Pacific Northwest, they retired early and joined a fun-loving group of gringos who live in "fifth-wheel" trailers on the sandy desert beach. They and their friends have little to do but party like spring-breakers. They go for day-long beach rides in their dune buggies and quads, sing karaoke, throw darts, hold potlucks, shoot pool, and play poker. They love to entertain.

They're generous with the locals. They hire their Mexican neighbors to build patios and decks, to paint their trailers, to fix their vehicles and plumbing. They've "adopted" the children of the village, and bring back toys and treats from their frequent supply runs to Yuma, Arizona.

My parents worked hard to earn their vacation retirement. My mother was an insurance underwriter and president of the Anchorage Women's Insurance Association. My step-dad was a food broker who entertained reps from companies such as Purina and Nestlé by taking them fishing in the Alaskan outback. Neither of them went to college. When I went off to school, I was on my own. Although I envy those who had help, maybe fending for myself fed my sense of autonomy, my independence. Nurture or nature? Who's to say?

Grandpa's Wheels, 2010
Watercolor, 4" x 6"

Quad, 2010
Watercolor, 8.5" x 12"

Baños, 2010
Ink wash, 8.5" x 12"

Dead Truck, 2010
Uniball Pen, 8.5" x 12"

Lunch Van, 2012
Uniball Pen, 8.5" x 12"

Botica, 2012
India ink, 8.5" x 12"

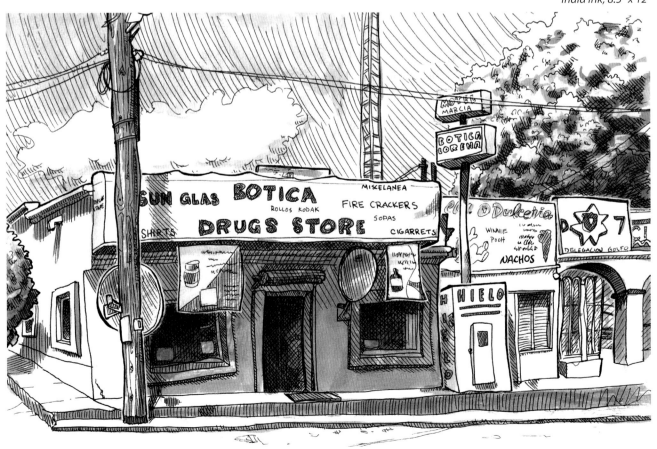

El Golfo

Carnival, 2010
Watercolor, 8.5" x 12"

The Point, 2010
Watercolor, 8.5" x 12"

Tienda Verde, *2012*
Watercolor, 8.5" x 12"

I parked my parents' quad across the street from this little green store. Packs of feral dogs sniffed my legs and trotted off looking for scraps that had fallen off the over-loaded fishing boats the night before. I'd already drawn the car when the shop owner came out and moved it, thinking I'd want a better view of his mural. He was clearly proud of it but I didn't know enough Spanish to ask him what the mural represented.

Cemetery, *2012*
Watercolor, 8.5" x 12"

El Golfo Gas Station, 2011
Watercolor, 8.5" x 11"

I drove the quad into town and parked in the only shade I could find, under a torn tarp stretched between some four-by-fours in the sand. Across the street was a scene I might not have drawn, but it was all I could see from my place in the shade.

    I leaned back in my seat and looked at the chaos of shapes until I figured out how to see it. **Hatchet,** by Gary Paulson, is the survival story I most enjoy reading with my fifth-grade students. In the book, a stranded and starving teenager can't see the perfectly camouflaged "fool birds" that are all around him. Only when he ignores their coloring and looks for their pear-shaped contours do they become visible.

    That's how I approach drawing a complicated scene—at first I just look for the contours, the edges of things.

Kalen, 2009
Ink wash, 8.5" x 11"

KALEN

Childhood shows the man, as morning shows the day.
        -Milton

Before my son was born I hadn't considered teaching as a career. As I researched school options for him, I realized I had strong opinions about education and child development in general. I knew what had worked and not worked well for me as a student. I took a few education classes in Broward County, Florida, where we were living. The more I learned the more interested I became. Being a teacher would also mean I'd be home for Kalen when he was home. I'd have great health insurance for the whole family.

But it would mean more debt. I had defaulted on my student loans and still owed more than $30,000. I was 32 years old. I was working for my wife's public relations company without a salary. With nothing to lose, I applied to the best two-year teacher certification program I could find—Seattle Pacific University—and filled out a financial aid form. I was surprised when I was accepted and approved for more loans. I moved our family to Seattle to go back to school. It was worth it. In two years, I had my own classroom.

Kalen Reading, 2010
Ink wash, 7" x 7"

I sang songs and read to Kalen as part of our nightly bed-time routine. He learned to read early and is an avid reader now. We waited in line at midnight for the new Harry Potter books. Then came Tom Clancy novels and in high school he began asking me for recommendations. Kalen's a political science major at Florida State University. He's followed my advice to work hard, keep his nose clean and his grades up. "Don't do as I did," I say, and so far he's listened.

Kalen Reading 2, 2009
Uni-ball, 7" x 11"

Kalen was so engrossed in his novel and I in my drawing that we didn't notice the ferry had docked until a crew member told us to get moving. We ran down to the car deck and drove off the empty ferry as waiting passengers glared at us for making everybody late.

Penny, 2009
Ink wash, 6" x 6"

Kalen and I were walking to the park with our baseball and gloves when I noticed this penny on the ground. Even without my glasses I could tell it was different somehow.

   "Kalen," I said, "What's the deal with this penny?"
He looked it over and said, "It's brand new. 2009."
   "But what's on the back?"
   "Oh. It's like a... it's a lumberjack reading a book."
   "What? How do you know it's a lumberjack?"
   "Because he's sitting on a log and his axe-thingie is laying next to him so he can read."
   "Why would he be reading?" I asked.
   "What, lumberjacks can't read?"
   "But what book would he be reading?"
   *"How do I know?" he laughed. "**Logging For Dummies.**"*

Unicycle, 2011
Watercolor, 8.5" x 11"

When Kalen was three, my wife took him back to Florida for a "family visit." I was deep into finals for my teaching certificate so I used the time to study. After three weeks I called to ask when Kalen was coming home. "He *is* home," she said. She would not return him to Seattle. I was blind-sided. An ugly legal battle followed. In the end, because of my teaching schedule, I would have Kalen during summer, winter and spring breaks, but fighting for time with my son added another 13K to my debt. I filed for bankruptcy.

Bankruptcy doesn't discharge student loans or personal debts, so Christmases were modest affairs. By living frugally and flipping a little fixer-upper house, I eventually paid off my debts and could afford nicer things for Kalen. One of his gifts each Christmas was a form of transportation. It was a challenge to keep finding something new. Over the years he got a scooter, a skateboard, a bike, a unicycle, a tour of Seattle on Argosy Cruises, and a plane trip to Hawaii. When he turned sixteen, I gave him money for a car and at seventeen, money for college. I think watching me do with so little for so long helped make Kalen financially sensible. He doesn't waste time or money.

A proud papa, my only concern is that he's very serious. He worries about his future and the future of the country. He worries about the people he loves. He's pretty tough on himself and doesn't think I push him hard enough. When he asks me for advice, I always say the same thing, "Make healthy choices, do well in school, but have fun."

Waiting At Seatac, 2009
Ink wash, 8.5" x 11"

Three times a year for sixteen years, Kalen flew round-trip from Florida to spend his summer, winter, and spring breaks with me in Seattle. (That's forty-eight full days of flying!) I'd arrive early to watch for his plane to land, and hug him goodbye at the gate when he left. This view became very familiar as I sat waiting for his plane to leave the tarmac.

Bed and Breakfast Caboose, 2010
Watercolor, 8.5" x 11"

Hanging with Kalen at Discovery Park, 2012
Watercolor, 8.5" x 11"

At The River, 2001
Cel-vinyl Animation Paint, 18" x 24"

I painted this cartoon map of the property for our family calendar. The original painting was sold at the auction we have each summer to pay the property taxes and upkeep.

Sharing a vacation schedule meant Kalen and I were free all summer to do whatever we wanted. My great-uncle left to my mother's side of the family a huge, undeveloped plot of land on the Green River. It's a special place, an hour southeast of Seattle, near Ravensdale, where we've held our yearly reunions since before I was born. Kalen and I spent our summers there, inner-tubing on the gentle rapids, exploring the woods and river banks. We built fires and cooked s'mores. We found deer bones, built stone dams, and climbed trees. Lucky, a local neighbor dog, followed us wherever we went and slept against the door of our tent.

My folks have a good relationship with Kalen. He likes to do all the things his grandfather enjoys: golfing, betting on the horses at Emerald Downs, playing Pinochle, following sports. I was always bookish and nerdy, with interests in musical theater and art, so I'm happy for my dad that he finally has someone to do these more typically "guy things."

Ravensdale Market, 2013
Watercolor, 8.5" x 12"

Family Reunion, 2011
Watercolor, 8.5" x 12"

My Irish family likes to party. They stay up late around the campfire, singing old Irish ditties, dancing, and telling stories. I'm the black sheep—early to bed, early to rise. I wake up and stoke the fire, still smoldering from the previous night's revelries and sit listening to the river and the birds. I sketched this view of one of the property's campgrounds while everyone was still asleep. My parents' trailer is on the right. Below is a view of the interior, drawn while we watched a DVD after roasting hot-dogs.

72 Hours, 2011
Watercolor, 8.5" x 12"

Bees, 2009
Uni-Ball Pen, 11" x 8.5"

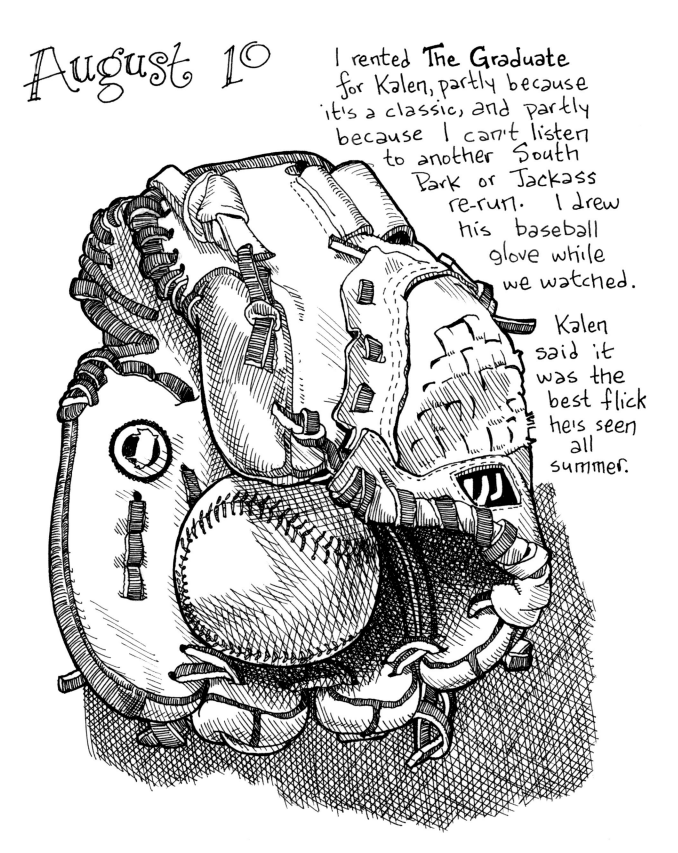

August 10

I rented **The Graduate** for Kalen, partly because it's a classic, and partly because I can't listen to another South Park or Jackass re-run. I drew his baseball glove while we watched.

Kalen said it was the best flick he's seen all summer.

The Graduate, 2009
Uni-Ball Pen, 11" x 8.5"

Barber Chair, 2009
Watercolor, 11" x 8.5"

Kalen's Haircut, 2010
Ink wash, 7" x 7"

Nola's Hair Salon, 2011
Ink wash, 8.5" x 11"

Emerald Downs, 2010
Ink wash, 8.5" x 11"

Each summer Kalen and I meet my parents at the race track, Emerald Downs. My mom brings a cooler of sandwiches, grapes, and Gatorade. We arrive early, set up tables at the front edge of the covered area, and play Pinochle until it's time to place our bets. Kalen watches his grandpa closely because he always seems to be ahead, though Gramps never shares his losing bets, so I suspect he's not as flush as he makes out. He talks a good game, though. Kalen and his grandpa huddle over the trade papers, underline relevant details, circle jockey's names, and draw arrows. They read the stats on the horses, consider the choice picks of the experts, and walk down to watch the horses load into the starting gate.

Before Kalen was old enough to place his own bets, I kept his winnings in one pocket and my money in another. Kalen wrote down his wagers for me to go make for him. I placed little bets for myself, something safe with a low yield but good odds. Kalen can place his own bets now, and when he wins big, he stops betting and goes home with a nice little bank roll. He's smart that way.

Between races my mind wanders. I space out. I might draw in my sketchbook but usually I just watch people—the odd couples, the sad old men, the pretty girls. I spend my meager winnings on a mocha and sit admiring my kid, who's way more together than I was at his age.

Kalen's Benjamin, 2009
Watercolor, 3.5" x 8"

We entered the Trivia Night Challenge at the Village Pub and our team won, thanks to Kalen. He knew the name of the planet that Darth Vader destroys in Star Wars, the number of rooms on the Clue gameboard, and the abbreviation for copper on the periodic table. Combined with his winnings from the track, Kalen pocketed his first Benjamin.

Eastlake Grill, 2010
Watercolor, 8.5" x 11"

Carnegie Library, 2011
Watercolor, 8.5" x 11"

Blockbuster, 2011
Watercolor, 8.5" x 11"

SEATTLE

To some extent, Seattle remains a frontier metropolis, a place where people can experiment with their lives, and change and grow and make things happen.

-Tom Robbins

I moved my family to Seattle in 1996 when I was thirty-four. I hadn't lived anywhere for more than a couple of years. Now, motivated by being a dad, I had a real job. I had health insurance. I settled down. I wanted Kalen to see me happy.

I can think of no place I'd rather live. The air is clean and water is everywhere. We bicycle and recycle. We have more bike lanes and walking trails than almost any other city. Seattle has one of the lowest obesity rates and the highest minimum wage. We've banned plastic grocery bags. Washington has legalized gay marriage and decriminalized marijuana, even for recreational purposes. Seattleites are rated the most educated and polite citizens in the United States.

Sure, it rains and the winters are long and dark and gloomy. But rain is conducive to art. We read, paint, play music, and write books. The lack of vitamin D didn't stop Jimi Hendrix or Jim Woodring, Bill Frisell or Bill Nye. Yes, traffic on the freeway is ugly. So what? Don't drive. I'm glad for the rain, or more people would be moving here and the traffic would be even worse. Come to think of it, forget what I said. Seattle is terrible. Do yourself a favor and don't come here. Go to Texas. I hear it's booming.

Gasworks 3, 2011
Ink wash, 12" x 9"

Gasworks 1, 2010
Watercolor, 11" x 8.5"

A grassy, 20-acre peninsula juts into Lake Union in North Seattle. The hilly park is dotted with huge rusting structures of rivets and steel like a set for a dystopian sci-fi film. The land was cleared in 1906 for a coal plant, but natural gas in the 1950's made the plant obsolete. Since 1975 the public park has been used for concerts, parties, rallies, and July Fourth fireworks displays.

Gasworks 2, 2011
Watercolor, 8.5" x 11"

To avoid commuting, I lived until recently in a small apartment (see page 15) only blocks from the school where I've taught for fifteen years. I could head south to the Myrtle Edwards Park trail along the Seattle waterfront and be downtown in minutes. I could go west one block and be in Discovery Park, five-hundred thirty-four secluded acres of protected tidal beaches, meadows, sea cliffs, forests, sand dunes, and streams overlooking Puget Sound, with views of the Cascades and the Olympic Mountains. I could ride my bike east along the forty-two mile Burke-Gilman-Sammamish trail all the way to our family property on Green River. Or, as I did almost every day, I could cross the Chittenden Locks into Ballard. The locks rise and fall to let boats pass from Lake Washington to the lower elevation to the west, while preventing the mixing of sea water from Puget Sound with the fresh water of the lakes. At night I could hear the sea lions fishing for salmon, and the great blue herons screeching like pterodactyls from their nests in the tall trees surrounding the locks.

Chittenden Library, *2012*
Ink wash, 8.5" x 11"

Chittenden Locks, *2008*
Watercolor, 10" x 8"

Seattle

Houseboats 1, *2011*
Ink wash, 8.5" x 11"

A friend and teacher, Elizabeth, rented a houseboat with her boyfriend Brandon near Gasworks Park on Lake Union. It's hard to find a spot to view the July Fourth firework display that isn't insanely crowded and chaotic. The view from their houseboat was unbelievable. I drew the two images on this page from their roof.

Houseboats 2, *2011*
Watercolor, 8.5" x 11"

Seattle is a city of water: salt water inlets and bays, fresh water lakes and rivers. Even short drives carry you near, over, or alongside bodies of water. Some neighborhoods are accessible primarily by ferry. Others are connected by bridges: drawbridges, floating bridges, toll bridges, viaducts, bascule, arch and truss bridges. Many of these bridges have been damaged by earthquakes, floods, or wayward vessels. An earthquake in 2001 caused two billion dollars in damages. My students and I felt the floor of our classroom heaving, and books fell off the shelves around us. Wayward ferries smash into docks and smaller craft. In 2013, part of Interstate 5 collapsed into the Skagit River, sending people and cars into the icy water. Fortunately, no one died.

I've always lived by the ocean: Kodiak Island and Anchorage, San Francisco, South Beach, FL. I've traveled to Nova Scotia, Hawaii, Acapulco, Bangkok, and Singapore. Only twice have I lived inland: two years in Fort Collins, CO., and less than one year in Jingdezhen, China. Both times I felt claustrophobic and trapped. I need to be near the ocean, at the edge of the landscape. It doesn't make logical sense. I don't own a boat. I can barely swim.

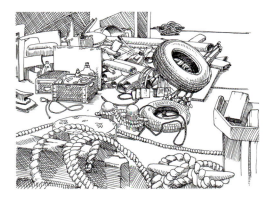

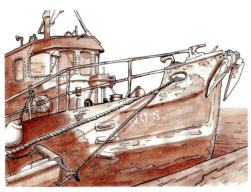

Kirkland Boat, *2011*
Ink wash, 8.5" x 11"

Sailing, 2010
Ink wash, 9" x 12"

I was invited to sail across the Puget Sound in November. I gamely tried to ignore my chattering teeth and stiffening fingers but after an hour or so the cold drove me below deck. I sat at the dining table with the captain's young son and drew pictures.

Sailboat Race, 2013
Watercolor, 9" x 12"

The boat below is the full-time home of Heidi and Kirk, whom I met through my TESOL (Teaching English to Speakers of Other Languages) classes. I drew this while standing near the helm during a casual sailboat race.

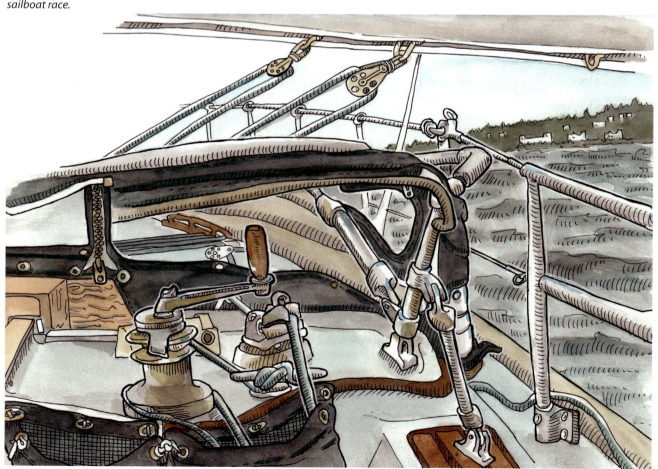

Brandon Drives, *2011*
Ink wash, 8.5" x 11"

Jeep Ride, 2013
Ink wash, 9" x 12"

Seattle 49

Homeless Camp, *2009*
Ink wash, 8.5" x 11"

Pioneer Square, *2009*
Ink wash, 8.5" x 11"

Seattle University, *2010*
Ink wash, 8.5" x 11"

Hi-Life Restaurant, *2009*
Ink wash, 8.5" x 11"

Center of the Universe, *2012*
Ink wash, 9" x 12"

Fremont Bridge, *2010*
Ink wash, 9" x 12"

Fremont Avenue, *2009*
Mixed Media, 10" x 8"

Fremont is a funky little North Seattle neighborhood on the Lake Washington Ship Canal. The rocket in the drawing on the previous page is made from the tail boom of a Fairchild C-119, a military transport aircraft developed during WWII. There's a 16-ft-tall statue of Vladimir Lenin, shipped here from Slovakia by a local art lover. The Fremont Troll is an 18-ft-high sculpture of steel and concrete, who is clutching an actual VW Beetle in one hand. Fremont hosts the annual Solstice Parade, which is really just an excuse for hundreds of people to ride their bikes through the neighborhood naked or wearing only body paint.

After Adobe and Google opened offices here, "The People's Republic of Fremont" became a bit more gentrified. Still, with its little shops and cafés, farmers market, and its proximity to Gasworks Park, it's a great place to walk, bike, and hang out.

Caught in a downpour near the end of a day-long bike ride, I sat with my mocha on the wrap-around porch of the old house that holds the *Fremont Coffee Company* (below) and sketched the view.

Fremont Coffee Company, *2010*
Ink wash, 9" x 12"

Ferry Dock, *2010*
Ink wash, 9" x 12"

Plugged-In Teen, *2010*
Brush Pen and Ink wash, 8.5" x 11"

My Man-Cave, *2008*
Ink wash, 8.5" x 11"

Ferry Commute, *2010*
Ink wash, 9" x 12"

On the ferry most people lock their cars and go up deck to look out the damp windows at the Puget Sound. It can be relaxing to watch the skyline recede or expand. Some mornings I stayed in the car to listen to National Public Radio and enjoy the peace and quiet before another day in my classroom.

For a new teacher, taking home about 2K a month, it would have taken me forever to pay off my student loans. I had to get creative. Across the Puget Sound in Bremerton, a conservative Navy town with little to offer a liberal artist and teacher such as myself, I found a little two-bedroom house on 1/4 acre lot. With my low salary, high debt, and terrible credit rating from bankruptcy and decades of unpaid student loans, I should not have been given a home loan. But this was 2003. Loans were being given to anyone with a pulse, with little concern for an ability to pay them off. They gave me 125K and I bought the house. I'm sure the bank assumed they'd own the house when I defaulted.

My little house became an art project—a second job. For five years I loved having my own little tiki-themed man-cave. I basked in the glow of home-ownership. My mortgage was $800 a month, but I paid more, $1000, $1200, whatever I had. One summer I challenged myself to go the entire month of August without spending a dime. I did it, using my time to work in the yard, go for runs, paint, and to play the guitar rather than to buy gas or to pay for entertainment. I refinished the hardwood floors and landscaped the yard. I grew vegetables. I planted a tree.

Five years later, tired of the commute and lonely in Bremerton, I sold the house, paid off my student loans, and moved back to Seattle with money in the bank. This was the summer of 2008. One month later the bottom fell out of the housing market. Banks failed and homeowners went "upside down." I had dodged a bullet. After 40-some years of hating the mail and ignoring the phone in case it was creditors, I was solvent. I resolved never to be in debt again.

Silhouette, 2012
India ink, 11" x 8.5"

JUST LOOKING

"If I were to draw, I would apply myself only to studying the form of inanimate objects," I said somewhat imperiously, because I wanted to change the subject and also because a natural inclination does truly lead me to recognize my moods in the motionless suffering of things.

-Italo Calvino, **If On a Winter's Night a Traveler**

Seattle is home to many cool vintage and antique stores. From tiny, crowded rooms in the owner's home (*Silhouette,* opposite), to vast consignment malls with numbered stalls (*Pacific Galleries,* page 73) it was easy to find interesting still-lifes all set up to draw. I asked a manager for permission first, because I didn't want to be in the way, arouse suspicion, or to be a distraction for shoppers. More importantly, I didn't want to be partway into a drawing and then told to leave, or at least to buy something already.

    I always brought my ear-buds and my own music, but if I was lucky, the shop played music I like, or at least something I could tolerate. Some stores played music that fit the theme of their merchandise. *Trove Vintage Boutique* (pages 58-61) played early sixties and soul music. *Atlas Vintage Mall* (pages 62-72) played strange, rarely heard albums from their vinyl collection. *Silhouette* played music that was so depressing (Barry Manilow, Helen Reddy, Glenn Campbell) that it was the perfect accompaniment to the leaking ceiling that dripped onto my sketchbook as I drew.

Space Oddity, 2013
Ink wash, 8.5" x 11"

Trove Cat, 2013
Ink wash, 8.5" x 12"

Trove Lighting, 2013
Ink wash, 8.5" x 12"

Trove Figurines, 2013
Ink wash, 8.5" x 12"

Trove Vintage Boutique is owned and operated by Cyrena Preszler and Sarah Leonard. I was drawn to the store by the artful window dressings and mid-century clothing designs near the front door. Many shops spread the inventory evenly throughout the store, but Trove is arranged into artful little vignettes. Each grouping makes a good subject for a drawing. I showed Cyrena my sketchbook and asked if I could sit and draw for an hour or so. *Trove Cat* (opposite, top) was the first drawing I did there. Normally I sit on my portable stool but I asked if I could sit on a couch that was for sale. I liked the angle, with the cat decanter on the steamer trunk and the desk in the background propped up on books to serve as their check-out counter. Cyrena and Sarah liked the finished drawing and used it as the banner on their website. The cat decanter sold the next day. I hope it was because someone saw the drawing.

I drew a few more times in the store and the ladies asked if I would be the featured artist for the upcoming Ballard Artwalk. Friends, family, and even some of my students and their parents came by to show their support and to buy a few prints.

I like to fill the page when I draw, but sometimes the scene doesn't fit the proportions of my sketchbook. With **Trove Figurines** *I took some creative license. I omitted a third shelf so I could fit in the watering can and coffee pot in the scene. One of the figurines was much smaller than the other but I decided to make them the same size. I also over-darkened the bottom left corner to help make the lamplight appear brighter.*

Trove Boutique, 2013
Watercolor, 8.5" x 12"
(Next page)

Just Looking

Fisherman's Storage Unit, 2009
Ink wash, 8.5" x 12"

This simple drawing was a small breakthrough for me. I'd just bought my portable drawing stool and was set up on a cold November day at Fisherman's Terminal near my apartment.

It looked as if someone had been evicted from his storage unit and all this junk was left outside the sliding doors. I didn't know what any of the junk was and that made it more interesting to draw. I saw it only as lines and shapes without names.

All my drawings up to then had been shaded with hatch lines, as in the drawing **Atlas Hatching** (right). Even with my gloves on I got too cold to finish all the little hatch lines I normally would have drawn. To hurry, I poured a little India ink into my drinking water and finished the shading with diluted Ink wash.

The finished drawing didn't look like anything I'd done before. I liked it, especially the little foreground bits.

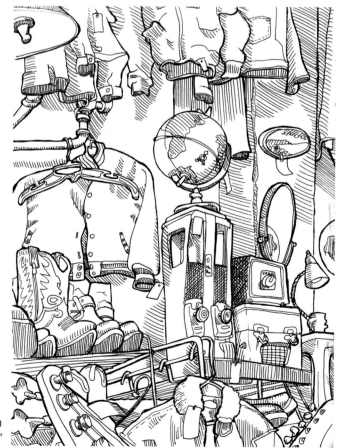

Atlas Hatching, 2010
Uni-Ball pen, 12" x 8.5"

On Timion's Fridge, 2012
Watercolor, 3" x 5.5"

Pink Atlas, 2009
Watercolor, 8.5" x 12"
(Below)

Pleased with the way the **Fisherman's Storage Unit** *came out, I tried the technique again, this time with magenta ink. I sought out a scene of clutter and detail and set up my folding stool inside a vintage mall. The shop was full of Christmas shoppers and this was my first time drawing in a crowd. I think being self-conscious and in a hurry helped. The drawing is loose and casual and is still a favorite of mine.*

Atlas Vintage Mall, 2009
Ink wash, 8.5" x 12"

This is an early vintage store sketch, drawn while customers shopped around me, occasionally buying the thing I was trying to draw. I wasn't yet comfortable being watched. Even so, I was pleasantly surprised that, even though I hadn't planned it out—I'd drawn no pencil guides or planned ahead—the scene turned out pretty much as I saw it. "A place for everything and everything in its place."

Deluxe Junk, 2010
Ink wash, 8.5" x 12"

Atlas Sled, 2012
Ink wash, 8.5" x 12"

Deluxe Junk, 2010
Ink wash, 8.5" x 12"

I had just recently met professor, marathon runner and artist, Dr. Jacqueline Helfgott. Jackie would be a big influence on me for the next three years and many of the drawings in this book were done on sketch outings together. At the time of this sketch I didn't know her well, so it was a pleasant surprise when, halfway through the drawing, she dropped by to say hello during her daily ten-mile run.

Just Looking

Atlas Mask, 2012
Ink wash, 8.5" x 12"

Atlas Coffee Table, 2012
Ink wash, 8.5" x 12"

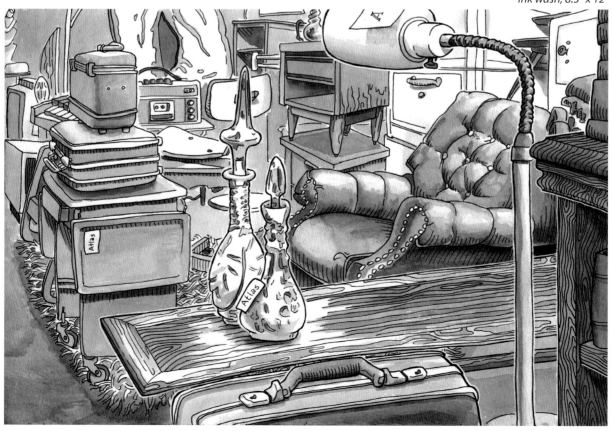

Atlas Ladder, 2011
Watercolor, 11" x 8.5"

On wet or cold days, I'll sit indoors listening to my ear-buds or the store's music if it's good. Atlas Vintage Mall is a consignment store in Fremont, with rooms for many different vendors to display their vinyl LPs, retro lunch-boxes, and 50s furniture. For every visit I can set up in a different part of the store and have a new scene to draw. By the time I've drawn my way around the different displays, the first ones have been rearranged and restocked with new oddities.

I've grown more comfortable drawing in public now. Only a few people stop and say anything. They nod their heads, comparing my drawing to the actual scene in front of us. Sometimes they talk about how they used to want to be artists and why they eventually gave it up. Sometimes they were discouraged by fiscally-minded parents or the insensitive comments of friends. Art seemed frivolous and unappreciated. Most often they say they quit because they just got out of the habit. Often the dream ended when college ended. After graduation, there were no more deadlines or due dates, no built-in audience. They remember sketching fondly though. Chatting with them always makes me feel fortunate that I never quit drawing. Never considered it.

Atlas Skates, 2012
Ink wash, 8.5" x 12"

Atlas Vintage Mall, 2012
Ink wash, 8.5" x 12"

Atlas Couch, 2012
Ink wash, 8.5" x 12"

Tamborine, 2012
Watercolor, 8.5" x 12"

Sometimes I'll begin a drawing with pencil. I lightly sketch geometric place-holders for the main elements: a quick cylinder for a bottle, a cube for a record player, or a sphere for a teapot. Occasionally I'll begin a drawing with no plan at all. In those cases drawing is like assembling a puzzle. I don't know ahead of time which objects in the scene will make the final cut.

For *Tamborine* (above), I began by drawing my own hand and the sketchbook and then moved clockwise to the bowl, the wine glasses, the bottle in the wicker cozy and its cork, and so on around the picture. If I drew something too big, the suitcases for example, then I omitted something else to compensate. Maybe there was an umbrella stand between the green suitcase and the desk, but including it would have pushed things too far to the right, crowding out the green shelves. So I left some things out. Who's to know? The same went for the slats on the floor or the number of books on the shelf. Without counting, I just focused on one thing at a time, teasing out the scene, selecting whatever seemed most interesting to include at the time. I made my way around the perimeter, making sure to draw the foreground objects first. I was pleasantly surprised by the way the pieces of the puzzle fit together.

Atlas Coat, 2012
Ink wash, 8.5" x 12"
(Next page)

Just Looking

Viking Lamp, 2012
Watercolor, 8.5" x 12"

Trying to build the contrast between the bright light and the shadows, I applied so many layers of ink-wash that the paper couldn't absorb any more. You can see where the ink pigment started to puddle just left of the chair.

The Neighbor's Things, 2010
Ink wash, 8.5" x 12"

Pacific Galleries, 2012
Watercolor, 8.5" x 12"

Pacific Galleries, 2012
Watercolor, 8.5" x 12"

The Seattle School District adopted new reading, spelling, and math programs in order to align with the national Common Core Curriculum. Pacific Galleries sits across the street from the Seattle School District central office, where we teachers met over the summer for professional development. I did the two drawings on this page during lunch-hour breaks.

Mort's Cabin, 2012
India ink, 8.5" x 12"

Jackie and I passed Mort's Cabin on Eastlake Avenue in North Seattle during our 7-mile runs around Lake Union. I was attracted by the warm glow coming from inside and by the interesting hand-made wooden furniture placed out on the sidewalk.

Operated by Darold Anderson, son of Mort, it's a crowded but beautiful little shop of Northwest-themed furnishings and accent items to give your home a rustic, log-cabin feel. The packed aisles barely accommodate a single shopper, let alone a sketcher with his own stool and a sketchbook on his lap. I asked Darold if there was a time when I might be able to sketch and not be in the way. He told me not to worry.

"Make yourself comfortable," he said. "Can I get you some tea?"

We had a pleasant chat and Darold took some pictures of me drawing in his shop for use on his website. When I finished we exchanged information and I asked if I could come and draw again.

"Any time," he said.

Mort's Cabin, 2013
Ink wash, 12" x 8.5"
(Opposite)

2nd Avenue (Beach), 2011
Watercolor, 12" x 8.5"

2nd Avenue, 2011
Ink wash, 12" x 8.5"

LONG BEACH

Let me be a free man—free to travel, free to stop, free to work.
   -Chief Joseph

My cousin Charles and his wife Lynn live, work and surf in Southern California. They let me crash with them during my spring vacations from teaching or when I'm passing through on my way to Mexico. Charles is an artist and designer for Quiksilver. Lynn is a photographer who also delivers for the Postal Service. While they work I explore the local neighborhood, sketching my way from coffee shop to café, running on the beach, or reading in the shade of a palm tree. I enjoy decompressing with them at the end of their long work days, sipping tea and sharing songs from our iTunes playlists. Although they are super busy, they generously spend their valuable free time driving to Joshua Tree or San Juan Capistrano, showing me the art galleries or hiking with me in the Hollywood Hills. I was sleeping on their couch when I got a job offer to teach English in China.

Lifeguard Shack, 2011
Watercolor, 8" x 12"

Long Beach

Charles' Cameras, 2011
Ink wash and Watercolor, various sizes

Korean Friendship Bell, 2011
Watercolor, 8.5" x 12"

Both Charles and Lynn are avid surfers and photographers, often shooting on film when most people have moved exclusively to digital. Charles has an impressive collection of working vintage cameras (opposite). One night, as we chatted in his living room, I drew one after the other, attracted to their clean lines and variety of styles.

Charles also has a great collection of original surfer art, signed prints, band posters, and art books. From my nest on the living room couch, I drew my view of their living room (below).

Charles has a weak spot for surfboards as well, and owns more boards than he can fit in his garage. During a tour of the Quiksilver campus where Charles works, Lynn noticed a dark surfboard propped across two walls of Charles' office cubicle.

"Charles," Lynn asked. "What is this?"

Charles said, "Um… that's a surfboard."

"I can see that. Would it be yours?"

No answer.

"Charles! We're saving for your overdue root canal, and you bought another surfboard?!" Lynn ran her hand along the edge of the board. "It *is* nice, though."

Chez Chaz, 2011
Watercolor, 8.5" x 12"

Charles Drives, 2009
India ink, 8.5" x 11"

This was drawn on the long drive to Joshua Tree. I'm lucky that I don't get motion sickness while bouncing around in the backseat of an SUV. Drawing accuracy goes out the window in favor of raw capture. When I'm old and shaking with palsy, I should still be able to draw with at least this amount of dexterity. Once we got to the park, Charles and Lynn hiked out of sight while I sat and drew the unusual bubble-shaped boulders and distant hills (below). It was dark before any of us wanted to leave.

Joshua Tree, 2009
Watercolor, 8.5" x 11"

Lynn Drives, 2009
India ink, 8.5" x 11"

It was Lynn's turn to drive for our hike to the Hollywood sign. I recognized the trails and views from movies and television shows such as **Men of a Certain Age** and **Episodes**. The Hollywood sign is fenced off to protect it from graffiti and suicide attempts. Police helicopters hover, yelling at teenagers who attempt to scale the fence. We ate lunch at the top with a view of LA in front of us and Burbank behind. On the way down, some Asian tourists asked us to take pictures of them jumping around in front of the sign and asked if we knew where to find the Batcave from the original TV series. We didn't know.

San Juan Capistrano, 2012
Ink wash, 8.5" x 11"

Long Beach

2nd Avenue Starbucks, 2010
Watercolor, 12" x 8.5"

Sun Tan, 2010
Ink wash, 12" x 8.5"

Jack In The Box, 2010
Ink wash, 12" x 8.5"

It might seem like an odd way to spend a vacation—sketching my way along 2nd Ave in Long Beach, California. But I'd been teaching the same grade, at the same school, in the same classroom, for thirteen years. That's a long time to be staring at the same four walls, day after day.

When my son was born I curbed my wanderlust and settled down. After thirty-some years of moving from city to city, school to school, job to job, I had become a responsible adult and bought a tie and a house and opened a 401K. I barely recognized myself. I owned a *lawnmower*.

But now my son was headed to college. My student loans were paid. I was single. Wandering around Long Beach I took a personal inventory and thought about the next phase. Walking around for a week in sunny Southern California had less to do with where I was, and more to do with where I wanted to go next. I'd never left the country. I didn't have a passport. But now I had possibilities. The Peace Corps wanted to send me to Micronesia. I also had an offer to teach English to college students in China. My freedom was a new pair of shoes that needed breaking in.

Scrap, 2010
Watercolor, 8.5" x 12"

El Burrito, 2009
Uni-Ball pen, 8.5" x 12"

Rae's Diner, 2010
Watercolor, 12" x 8.5"

Long Beach

DOWNSIZING

"The things you own, end up owning you."
  -Chuck Palahniuk, **Fight Club**

I like being self-contained, living minimally with only what I can carry. As a kid, tales of survival and resourcefulness, like *Robinson Crusoe* and *The Swiss Family Robinson* suggested a truer, in-the-moment lifestyle than one coasting in complacency. For my students, I designed an integrated science, reading, and history unit around Thor Heyerdahl's 101 days on the Pacific Ocean on the *Kon-Tiki*, a raft no bigger than our classroom.

As a kid I was content with my books and records in my bedroom. Even today I like to be able to see everything I own all from one vantage point. I love to draw clutter, but I don't like living in it.

As I prepared to move to China, I was surprised by how much junk had accumulated in my little apartment. I took the opportunity to purge. By coincidence I came across *The 100 Thing Challenge* by Dave Bruno, a book about limiting your physical possessions. Except for my favorite art-books, my journals, and some paintings, I sold, tossed, or gave everything away. For an end-of-the-year thank-you gift, my students' families gave me luggage, which was perfect as I didn't own so much as a duffel bag. I didn't stop downsizing until everything I owned fit into my two new suitcases.

Clutter, 2011
Watercolor, 8.5" x 12"

Ballast, 2011
Watercolor, 8.5" x 12"

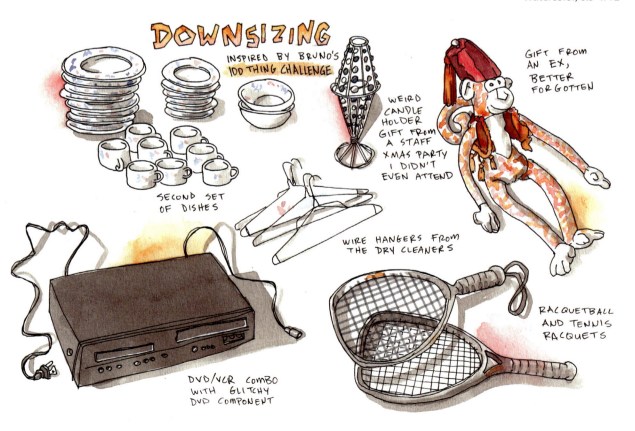

Downsizing, 2011
Watercolor, 8.5" x 12"

Easy Street/Happy Pride, 2011
Watercolor, 8.5" x 11"

I once had an impressive collection of vinyl albums that I treated with kid gloves and a lot of TLC. I owned every record by Neil Young, Talking Heads, Frank Zappa, and Pink Floyd, just to name a few. Like many collectors, I sold the records and gradually rebuilt my music library with CDs.

Now, once again, I found myself handing over box after box to a young man covered in tattoos and piercings. I sat across the street and drew while he inspected and appraised each disc, popping open the jewel case to look for scratches I knew he wouldn't find. As "mint" as my CDs were, I was still paid pennies on the dollar. Oh, well. A small price for freedom.

Hawaiian Shirts, 2011
Watercolor, 8" x 10"

88   Now Where Was I?

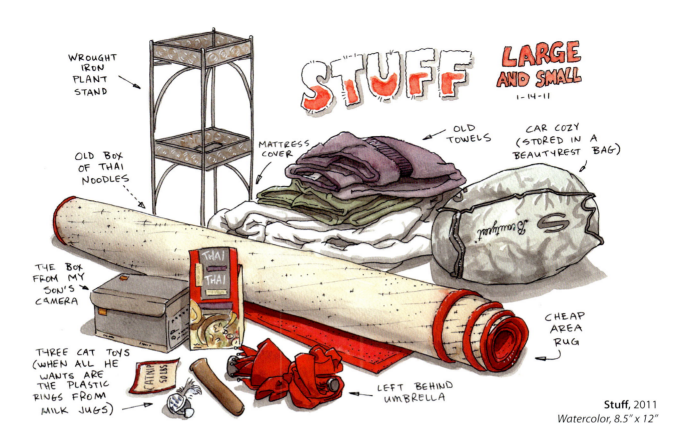

Stuff, 2011
Watercolor, 8.5" x 12"

Kitchen Klutter, 2011
Watercolor, 8.5" x 12"

Painting Supplies, 2010
Ink wash, 12" x 8.5"

I'd moved from a one-bedroom unit into a two-bedroom unit in the same building so I'd have space to set up an oil painting studio. Over two years, I finished and sold some large oil paintings and had several shows. But painting is much more dependent on space, time, and supplies than sketching. I didn't want to store all that stuff for the year I'd be living in China, only to return to dried-out paint tubes and brushes with bent and splayed bristles. The oil paints, canvases, brushes and mediums were probably worth close to $2000. William, the manager of my building, bought the whole collection (opposite page) for $400. The enlarger (the one in the box, not the cheap one on the music stand) cost more than that by itself. When I caught the plane to China, I left an apartment full of furniture, dishes, clothes, and shelves and shelves of miscellaneous junk. William had to sort it all out. Letting him have such a deal on all this stuff only lessened a little the guilt of leaving him such a mess.

Palmwood Tikis, 2010
Ink wash, 7" x 10"

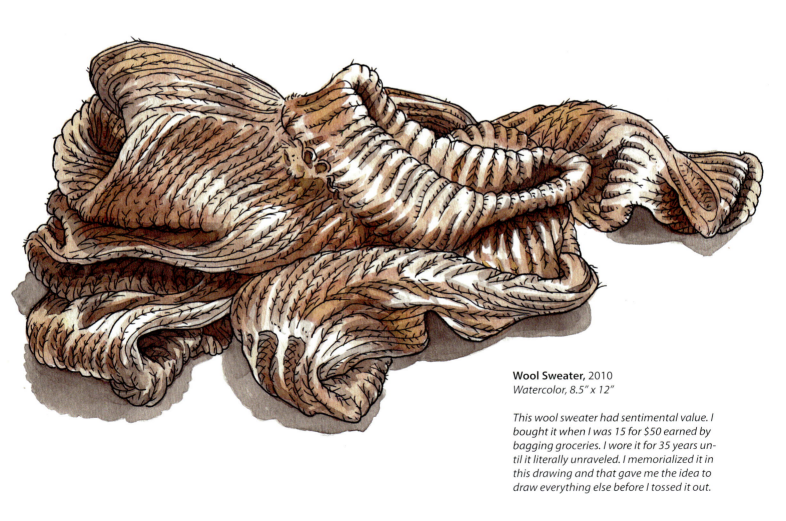

Wool Sweater, 2010
Watercolor, 8.5" x 12"

This wool sweater had sentimental value. I bought it when I was 15 for $50 earned by bagging groceries. I wore it for 35 years until it literally unraveled. I memorialized it in this drawing and that gave me the idea to draw everything else before I tossed it out.

Shoes, 2009
India ink, 8.5" x 12"

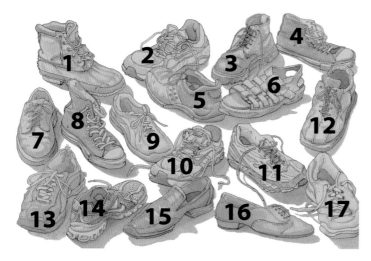

1. Cheap snow boots. Good for 5th-grade camp.
2. New Nikes. Bought for Sunday's 8K race.
3. Doc Marten's. Bought in '96.
4. Black Converse High-tops. My students like it when I wear them with suits.
5. Comfy Clarks for work. Too-slippery shoelaces always come untied.
6. Summer sandals. Rarely worn.
7. Boring work shoes.
8. Red Converse. Kalen wanted them and they were 2-for-1.
9. Bowling-style shoes. Slightly chewed on by a date's dog.
10. Last year's running shoes.
11. Kalen's running shoes.
12. Italian dress shoes. Make my feet look big.
13. Older pair of the same shoes as #9.
14. Old running shoes for going in the river.
15. Metrosexual slip-ons. Kalen calls them my "urban look."
16. Old dance shoes for crowded ballrooms where I'll be stepped on.
17. 8-yr-old Skechers, rarely worn.

Shoes Redux, 2009
India ink, 8.5" x 12"

For a guy who spent the first 36 years of his life wearing sneakers, I was surprised to see how many pairs of shoes I'd acquired, and the drawings on these two pages show only one shoe from each pair! Even accounting for special-use shoes—rock climbing, dancing, snow-shoveling, etc.—it's ridiculous that anyone would have this many.

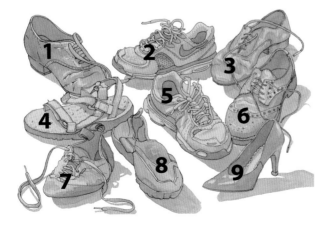

1. New Salsa shoes with felt soles.
2. Kalen's old running shoes.
3. Older Salsa shoes with too-slippery soles.
4. Summer sandals with straps that hurt.
5. Really old running shoes.
6. Expensive brown dress shoes that don't go with anything.
7. Climbing shoes for Vertical World Gym.
8. Water socks for Green River.
9. Left-behind by a former girlfriend.

Tiki Kitsch 2010
Watercolor, 8.5" x 11"

Mugs that came with Polynesian drinks, souvenirs from students after Hawaiian vacations, shot cups, a vase that once held Lucky Bamboo, a clay vessel that was a demo from an art lesson, and a cannibal bobble-head.

    I walk a fine but meandering line between the Puritan work ethic of my Irish Catholic upbringing and the desire to live off the grid—to labor only as needed to procure food and shelter. Each night I review the day and regret any wasted time. I make to-do lists for tomorrow and vow to complete my checklist. I don't own a television or go to the movies because time is too valuable. While running or exercising at the gym, I work on projects in my head. (I composed this paragraph while in the shower.)

    On the other hand, I spend hours every day just walking around town or riding my bike along Seattle's bike trails. I draw for hours without moving. I welcome boredom. I feel self-contained, complete, and wanting for nothing: no car or money, no phone or computer.

    I ride my bike along the waterfront with a song in my head:

> If I could make a wish, I think I'd pass.
> Can't think of anything I need.

It's my version of living on a deserted island, eating bananas and coconuts, beach-combing, drinking rainwater and whittling tikis.

Seattle Language School, 2010
Watercolor, 8.5" x 12"

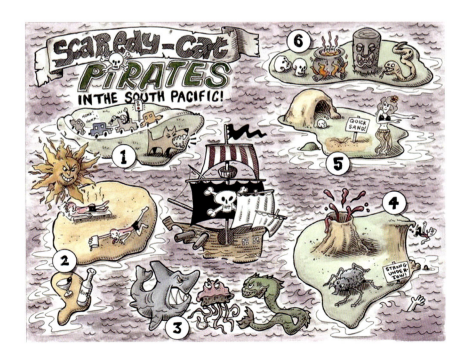

Scaredy-Cat Pirates!, 2010
Watercolor, 11" x 14"

I applied to the Peace Corps and asked to be sent to the South Pacific. I created this Pirates board game while enrolled at the Seattle School of TESOL (Teaching English to Speakers of Other Languages). Shortly after I completed the program, I was offered a job teaching English in China, which didn't require the certificate. I wasn't expected to know any Chinese but I enrolled anyway at the **Seattle Language School (above)** and took several months of Mandarin.

Haibo, 2011
Watercolor, 8.5" x 12"

A local family salvaged these giant mascots from the 2010 World Expo in Shanghai. They guard a small gate that leads to a pond traversed by a suspension bridge to nowhere. In the distance are the ubiquitous cranes and scaffolds of construction sites.

Hutian Temple, 2011
Watercolor, 12" x 8.5"
(Opposite)

Mosquitoes had me for dinner as I drew this tiny temple hidden in the woods at Hutian, the first state-preserved kiln site, dating from 907 A.D. Porcelain is a Chinese invention, known in the West as simply "China." Jingdezhen is known as the Porcelain Capitol of the World.

JINGDEZHEN

To do anything in this world worth doing, we must not stand back shivering and thinking of the cold and danger, but jump in, and scramble through as well as we can.
 -Sydney Smith

I left Seattle feeling self-congratulatory and brave. I'd never traveled out of North America, and there I was, not visiting as a tourist, but *moving to China*. I fantasized about being an international man of mystery, a liason between cultures, fluent in Chinese, smuggling out drawings of places where cameras were forbidden, and maybe an exotic affair.

But when I stepped off the plane and was greeted by thick, gray-green air and shoulder-to-shoulder crowding, I found myself holding my breath. The incessant and deafening honking of cloud-belching vehicles unnerved me, and when I saw the room I was to live in, I had to steel myself by remembering why I'd left clean, green Seattle and an established career in education: I wanted to be pushed out of my comfort zone, forced to grow.

My time in China was defined by extreme contrasts. I arrived sweating in 80% humidity, but in a few months I'd be sleeping in my wool hat and gloves. I sketched ancient, culturally-unique structures just before they were demolished to make way for cheap and hastily erected condos and office buildings. Friendly shouts of "Waiguoren! Hallo-o-o!" greeted me whenever I explored the city, but my six months of intensive Mandarin classes didn't help me connect with anyone beyond a practical level. My attempts to speak the language were met with amused smiles. "It okay. Engrish prease."

Gao Ling, 2010
Watercolor, 8.5" x 12"

Gao Ling was a 21-year-old design major at the Jingdezhen Ceramic Institute where I taught Oral English to mostly female freshmen and sophomores. She was well-served by her curiosity and confidence. Unlike most of my students, she wasn't shy about asking me personal questions.

"So how long since you no longer married?" she asked on our weekly five-kilometer walk to **San Bao** (opposite).

"14 years."

"Really? So long! And you didn't get married again?" She walked slowly, thinking it over. "After a divorce," she said, "and you feel sad, Chinese men take maybe one, two years, then get married again. They want to be with someone."

"Well, I've had girlfriends… ."

"In China I think we would consider that married," she said.

"So when you asked me if I was married again, that's not really what you were asking me, was it?"

She laughed.

I was asked often where my wife was. Being single at my extreme old age—I was forty-nine—aroused suspicion. One of my few male students asked if I was recovering from a previous relationship.

"You Westerners talk a lot about freedom and independence," he said. "But over here, if you stay single after college, we just assume it's because you are either broken or unlovable."

Ric Swenson was my high school art teacher and he suggested, 35 years later, that I teach in China. On my second day he introduced me to Gao Ling. She served as my translator, showed me how to find the things I needed, took me to interesting sketching locations, and gave me tours of local art studios and galleries. Although extremely poor and with none of the guanxi (social influence) that the Chinese use to help secure a future, she was consistently charming and optimistic. I drew this in Ric's studio while Gao Ling etched Chinese characters onto his pots.

San Bao Creek, 2010
Watercolor, 8.5" x 12"

The San Bao artist's colony was founded in the mid-1990's as an international ceramic art center where artisans meet to exchange the culture, arts and crafts of China. It's located in a scenic valley down a long dirt road that winds through rice fields and past water-powered hammer mills used for crushing the Chinastone that can be used for exceptionally thin but sturdy porcelain pottery.

San Bao, 2010
Watercolor, 8.5" x 12"

China WC, 2010
Watercolor, 8.5" x 12"

Student Bath House, 2010
Watercolor, 12" x 8.5"
(Opposite)

Students sleep six to a room without hot water. To shower, they carry plastic buckets of toiletries and a change of clothes across campus to this Bathing House. The showers are heated by burning reclaimed lumber, still covered with plaster and paint, so dark smoke billows from the chimneys all day, onto the basketball courts and into our open windows. From my window at night I could see small groups of students in pajamas and flip-flops, with wet hair and towels over their shoulders heading back to their crowded dorms.

Using the Asian-style bathroom took some getting used to. While showering I had to watch my footing so I didn't step in the hole and twist my ankle in the squat toilet. The first time I turned on the water it came out so hot I scalded myself. There was no shower curtain so the water went everywhere and out the drain hole below the sink. Towels and toilet paper left in the room became soaked and useless. One morning, up at 5:00 to catch a bus for my physical—required for the resident work visa—I stood under the nozzle only to discover that the water was turned off every night until 6 a.m. On the bright side, the morning view from my fourth floor bathroom window was gorgeous: a large lotus pond and the sun rising over the eastern hills.

Shower View, 2011
Watercolor, 5" x 8"

Massage, 2010
Watercolor, 12" x 8.5"
(Opposite)

As I drew these signs a crowd gathered on the sidewalk. Children playfully stood in my sightline until their parents pushed them out of the way. I asked my students what the signs said and they told me one advertised foot massages and the smaller one was for a restaurant.

The Jingdezhen Pottery Studio is an international ceramics center focusing on the development and enrichment of ceramics in China and abroad. Every Friday night, there is a lecture, open to the public, by a visiting sculptor, potter, or ceramicist. I was invited to prepare a forty-five minute presentation about my background, education, process, and anything else I wanted to share. It was hard to decide what to include in the lecture, especially because I knew nothing about ceramics. I didn't sleep well Thursday night, building and rebuilding my slide show.

Friday evening, hundreds of stone-faced students and instructors filled the hall. They provided a translator. I didn't factor in how much longer it takes to say in Chinese what I could say quickly in English. When I finished and it was time for the Q&A, the evening's host said, "Since this went a little long, let's save the questions for the reception at the café."

"I went over?" I asked. "By how much?"

"Ninety minutes," he said.

I was embarrassed and afraid I had seemed self-absorbed and indulgent. At the meet-and-greet everyone was kind and complimentary but I knew they wouldn't have complained even if I had worn out my welcome.

Artist Lecture, 2010
India ink, 8.5" x 12"

Jingdezhen

Urban Homes, 2010
Watercolor, 8.5" x 12"

Old Campus, 2010
Watercolor, 8.5" x 12"
(Opposite top)

Gao Ling said I should draw this red brick building on the older of the two campuses. It once housed the original school, founded in 1909.

Park Bridge, 2010
Watercolor, 8.5" x 12"
(Opposite below)

Gao Ling called this green space between some apartments "her park." While I sketched this little bridge, she stretched in the grass like a cat, ignoring her textbook and singing softly to herself.

I paid a woodworker to build two tables for me: one large enough to serve as a table and a smaller bedside stand, for 280 yuan (about $40). A few days later, my phone rang but I couldn't understand who it was and twice hung up. Gao Ling called the number for me and explained that my custom tables were finished. The carpenter found a very old rickshaw-puller to cart them the mile to my dorm. I offered to help him carry the heavy wooden furniture up the four flights of stairs to my room, but he waved me off, hoisted both tables onto his back, and carried them up alone. When I handed him 60 yuan (about $10), he said that he didn't have change. Gao Ling helped me explain, "It's for you," she said. "Keep it." He seemed reluctant, almost insulted, but he nodded and left.

When I told Olga, a Spanish calligraphy student, she said that I shouldn't over-tip the locals because it reinforces the notion that all foreigners are rich and can be charged "foreigner prices" instead of "local prices." But foreigners *can* afford to pay more, I thought. This very old man was worth a lot more to me than the $2 he expected.

Wall of Discards (Linework), 2010

Wall of Discards (Ink wash), 2010

Wall of Discards, 2010
Watercolor 8.5" x 12"

Sometimes I come across a scene that presents itself as a subject and I immediately get to work. Other times I'll wander around for hours with my folding stool in my satchel without being inspired to stop and draw. I like to walk, and even though I may see something interesting, sometimes the momentum of my stroll won't be interrupted, and I'll just keep moving.

I look for several qualities in a subject. First, there has to be enough detail and complexity to keep me interested for the hour or two that I'll be sitting and studying the shapes, colors, contours, and shading. I prefer there to be a clear foreground, middle ground, and background. But occasionally the amount of detail will engage me even if the image is fairly flat. To help create a sense of depth, I'll set up my stool close to one end of the wall and draw at an angle to give a little perspective to an otherwise flat scene.

Because I work in pen, I draw the foreground first and work my way back with a line drawing. People often refer to my work as "cartoony." The word *cartoon* originated in the Middle Ages and is from the Italian "cartone" and Dutch "karton." The word originally described a preparatory drawing for a painting or a fresco. Contemporary comics and animation emphasize contours, so now the word "cartoon" has a childish, "lowbrow" connotation. So be it.

The second stage is sculpting the forms by painting in the shadows. I use thin layers of diluted India ink applied with a brush. For **Discards** (opposite page), I left the left side of the wall unfinished to suggest some atmospheric perspective. Since objects farther away are perceived through more air, they look paler and less defined. I darkened the tree on the left side to bring it forward to contrast with the lighter, distant wall on the left side of the drawing. Sometimes I'm satisfied at this stage and stop, but when I decide to color a painting, I apply very thin washes of watercolor over the *grisaille,* French for "monotone under-painting," so the shading still shows through. As I tell my art students, "Black and white does the work; color gets the credit."

Student Work, 2010
Watercolor, 8.5" x 12"

Outside a communal studio for students, a girl with the English name Deer sat beside me and shared her discontent with the Communist Party. She'd hoped to join, but was put off by the "enforced patriotism." She said it was obviously "brain-cleaning," but there were professional and financial advantages to being involved in the party. She, like many of her peers, felt helpless and resigned.

The West Virginian Exchange Students' Studio, 2010
India ink, 8.5" x 12"

Each fall, West Virginia University offers a 12 credit study and travel program in Jingdezhen so students will have the opportunity to study with some of China's most prominent teachers and ceramic artists.

When they arrived on campus, boisterous and fraternal, I felt that my desert island had been invaded. I was possessive of my position as the token Westerner in the city. I introduced myself to the West Virginians and found that a care package from home had been sitting in their studio for weeks. The local post office assumed any American must be part of this exchange program.

The West Virginians threw a costume party for Halloween. I had seen the Chinese freshmen going through the required military drills in blue camouflage, so I borrowed a uniform from a student. The largest one we could find was still uncomfortably tight. I wondered if an American wearing the blue camouflage uniform of the communist party would be seen as disrespectful, but no one complained. They wouldn't have, of course. Halloween night, dozens of my students attended to stand silently along the walls watching the Americans drink and dance in our costumes: roller derby queens, Fred Flintstone, ET, a zombie. When I asked my students why they came only to stand against the wall and watch, they explained that they'd come for "the show." When I said it was a party, not a show, they asked, "Then why are you all in costumes?"

I drew this collection of left-behind pottery after the West Virginians went home, leaving me as the city's sole "laowai" once again.

I have a fondness for mochas and longed for a little place to sit with a good cup of joe to read and respond to my students' journals. I could find nothing resembling a coffee shop in all of Jingdezhen. The restaurants—loud, hot, and full of smokers—did not encourage loitering, and the sight of a foreigner sitting alone reading or writing drew too much attention for me to concentrate on my work.

"Why you alone?" they'd ask. Sitting by myself, they explained, was a sign of depression. "Bu hao! No good! Don't be sad!"

The Ceramic Institute paid Gao Ling to ride the bus with me three hours to Jiujiang, a city of 5 million people, to get my required physical. Eating lunch in the city, I saw "*mocha*" listed on the menu and ordered one for each of us. Gao Ling raised her eyebrows at the expense, but I promised her it would be worth it. It wasn't. We were served lukewarm black coffee that reminded me of the free sludge you drink while waiting for your car at Jiffy Lube.

Back in Jingdezhen, I saw a woman walking with a to-go coffee cup. I knew enough Mandarin to ask where she got it, and she gestured down a side street to ***You You Ka Fei Shu Ba*** (Coffee Shop and Book Bar, below). They made a hot mocha worthy of any Seattle hipster barista. This well-stocked café made me feel at home, and it became my regular haunt. The owner, a young man from Beijing, spoke excellent English and played contemporary vocal jazz by Johanna Wang and my favorite classics by Joni Mitchell.

The owner's two puppies had free reign of the place, curling up at my feet as I worked. They grew quickly and were obviously well-cared for—a stark contrast to the mangy, bone-thin mutts that rummaged through the garbage outside. I got used to them sighing under my chair. One day there was only one puppy, so I asked where the other one was.

"He's dead," the owner shrugged. "It happens."

I spent a lot of time at You You. The day I left China, I gave him this drawing as a thank-you.

You You Ka Fei Shu Ba, 2010
Watercolor, 8.5" x 12"

Gallery Bar, 2010
Watercolor, 8.5" x 12"

The Pottery Workshop had a small café connected to the art gallery. After the Friday lecture, the crowd would meet here for a reception and drink Tsingtao, the most popular dark beer made in China. Not a beer drinker myself, I asked for a cocktail and was given a martini made with Baijiu, a "white wine" that is actually a distilled liquor about 60% alcohol. "My invention!" the bartender said. It was undrinkable. Instead, I indulged in the mini-Snickers chocolate bars they sold at the register.

Korean Restaurant, 2010
Watercolor, 8.5" x 12"

Green Restaurant/Angel Paradise, 2010
Watercolor, 8.5" x 12"

The Master's Studio, 2010
Watercolor, 8.5" x 12"

Entry Gate, 2010
Watercolor, 8.5" x 12"

I taught classes for only a few hours each day, with Fridays and weekends to myself—plenty of time to explore the city. Though I always carried my sketchbook and pens, I often spent hours just taking it in, interacting with the locals, observing the culture. As I fell into a routine, I began to miss feeling like a stranger in a strange land. Even though I was on the other side of the world, and I was treated, in some ways, like a minor celebrity, it all started to feel routine and predictable. Out of boredom, I began to take more and more risks.

I'd been advised not to discuss politics, religion, or sex, but curiosity got the better of me. I had come all this way, after all. I wanted to know more about the culture. Some students were eager to share; some almost desperate to air their political grievances and social frustrations. But most students were shy. One student said, "I don't like to talk about our government. It makes me ashamed." By giving the students journals and a few minutes at the end of each class to write, I got information I couldn't get face to face.

Did students study the history of China? *The good parts.* How did people feel about Chairman Mao? *He was 70% right and 30% wrong.* Was the one-child rule strictly enforced? *Only in the cities. But rich families can pay a fine and have more children as a sign of status.* What about Taiwan and Tibet? *They are part of China, period.* Is there still animosity toward the Japanese? *Yes. But we like South Korea because there we will get plastic surgery to make our faces thinner.* Has religious worship died out completely? *Mostly, but some old people remember it.* Is sex education taught in schools? *Never.* Why do I not see any couples on the streets—no one holding hands or hugging? *It's private.* Do students date? *What does that mean?*

Although the internet was heavily censored, most students spent all their free time on-line, chatting with friends on Baidu, China's sanctioned version of Facebook, or emailing each other through their qq accounts. I learned from an unusually candid female student that gay-male porn was popular among the girls. By illegally installing a VPN, "virtual private network," they worked around the government censors and were able to access the internet unchecked.

Wo de Jiā, 2010
Watercolor, 8.5" x 12"

Along the Nanhe River, a tributary of the Yangtze, every square foot of land between the water and the houses was used for gardening. Narrow dirt pathways divided the uneven earth into a patchwork of vegetable beds, like a rumpled green quilt. There were no fences or signs to denote property lines. I had the sense that it was shared or farmed collectively. The greenery stretched on for miles. I sat between rows of lettuce to draw the wonky geometry of the houses (above).

An elderly woman appeared at my side and watched me work. She talked with enthusiasm, pointing at my drawing and then up to the houses.

I apologized in Mandarin, "Duibuqi, wo bu dong." *Sorry, I don't understand.*

But she went on, pointing at the building under the water tower.

Finally, I understood the phrase, "Wo de jia." *My home.*

The week before I left Jingdezhen, I went back to the river to sketch the gardens. A construction crew was laying pipeline along the Nanhe, and the gardens had been torn out. Bare dirt and tractors sat where the vegetables had been. Had the farmers depended on those crops for food? Did they sell them for income? Had they been compensated? Had they even owned the land to begin with?

Google Earth still shows the gardens, but they're gone now.

Tagged For Demolition, 2010
Watercolor, 12" x 8.5"
(Opposite)

I packed American-style lunches of sandwiches, apples, chips, and cookies, and walked with a student to San Bao for a picnic lunch. In a rare public display of affection, she took my hand and didn't let go all day. Lulu, "Deer" in Mandarin, explained to me that the circular red tag near the front door of this building indicated that it would be torn down. The family that was living in it came out to watch me sketch but refused to let me photograph them.

114   Now Where Was I?

Neighbors, 2010
Watercolor, 8.5" x 12"

All of my sophomore students had chosen English names. Many were based on common nouns: *Deer, Cloud, Sky.* Three girls were named *Apple.* Also popular were adjectives such as *Juicy, Blue,* and *Sweet.* An earnest young man who would become a friend (and the only male besides me invited to Lulu's birthday party) was a fan of Thomas Edison and signed his name "Edson." In her class journal, one student explained her chosen name this way:

> *Mr. Steve, I want to explain my English name to you. My name is so easy to remember. It is "And." At first you may be amazed. In Chinese, "And" means "He." It relates to peaceful and harmonious. I am a anti-war person, so the name can always remind me. Besides, in English, "And" is a conjunction. It can conjunct some different or contrast things together. I want to be a bond between anything."*

Some of the freshmen wanted me to suggest names for them. I asked them to pronounce their Chinese names, and then I said the names that occurred to me. Wang Min wrote to me in her journal:

> *I am so honored that I got the name of Wanda that you think it for me. I like it very much. Thank you, my dear teacher.*

From my dorm window, I could see a labyrinthian neighborhood of uneven narrow paths and tall cement walls. With my folding stool and sketchbook, I went to explore it. In the center of the maze was a public atrium with a few trees growing from the dirt floor. I sketched in the shade as a dozen young children gathered to clown and climb on the low walls, hoping to get into the drawing. When a woman hurried out to remove the row of drying laundry, I muttered, "Oh, no." One of the young boys heard me and yelled in vain for her to leave it. The reddish garment hanging on the left was all I captured before she carried it inside.

Pottery Studio, 2010
Watercolor, 8.5" x 12"

Gao Ling and her friend Fish went with me to sketch this building. It seemed everyone in Jingdezhen could draw. They shrugged off my compliments, saying it doesn't provide a living so why bother? A young boy I tutored was not impressed with my sketchbooks.
 "I think it is boring," he said. "In the time it takes, you could do something more interesting."
 "Like what?" I asked.
 "Like watch television," he said. "Or play video games."

Garden Gate, 2010
Watercolor, 8.5" x 12"

On a walk, I came to this vegetable garden near the edge of campus and let myself in. Asking for permission to go inside the many walls and fences to draw the interesting things inside was awkward and unnecessary. If I unfolded my stool and opened my sketchbook, a curious resident might watch over my shoulder for a while, but no one ever complained or questioned me about it.

Potter's House, 2010
Watercolor, 8.5" x 12"

The owner of this studio gave me sugarcane and asked if he could photograph me holding his vases. Earlier, a man had offered me 300 yuan to teach for one hour at his private school so he could take pictures to imply his school employed Western teachers. I had declined. So now I assumed this potter was going to create a brochure or website showing that his pottery was in demand by wealthy foreigners. This time I replied, "Shì de, dāngrán." ("Of course.")

Fruits Love Fruits, 2010
Watercolor, 12" x 8.5"

Eating was a problem for me. Even if I had known how to cook, I had no kitchen. The walls of restaurants dripped black with the residue of cooking oil. I couldn't stomach the slimy, fried eels and barely dead slippery things the restaurants sold. Unfamiliar black serpents audibly writhed in bowls on the floor, waiting to be consumed. Even salads had tentacles and things I didn't recognize with eyeballs attached.

I limited myself to two or three restaurants I trusted. One restaurant, literally translated, was called *Fruits Love Fruits* (opposite). For 7 yuan, about $1, I could get a good-sized bowl of Jiang Bao Ji Ding, Kung Pow Chicken without the nuts. I learned to ask for it without the red hot chili peppers, "*Bu yao heng la jao.*" It was a good day if I remembered to bring napkins because paper products, too rare and expensive to be left on the tables, were not provided. I ate out less and less and got more than a little melancholy.

I longed for a roast beef sandwich or a Caesar salad with blackened salmon. I ate a lot of raw fruits and vegetables—cucumbers and apples. I'd been warned that the water in the skins would make me sick, so I peeled them with a new but disappointingly dull potato peeler.

The first month, I ran each morning on the school's track, but because of the poor air quality, I stopped. I felt tired and sluggish. I worried about my health.

One night, lonely and bored, I ventured out for something hot and ordered a bowl of chicken soup. (Locals were surprised I could use chopsticks. They had been told Westerners couldn't manage them, although China imports their chopsticks from a small town named Americus, near Atlanta, Georgia.) Now where was I? Oh, yes, I was picking the bones out of my soup. I plucked out a large triangular mystery chunk. I turned it in my chopsticks, examining it closely until I recognized the eyes and beak of a chicken's head.

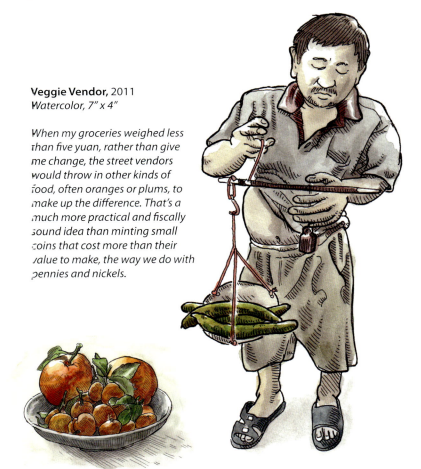

Veggie Vendor, 2011
Watercolor, 7" x 4"

When my groceries weighed less than five yuan, rather than give me change, the street vendors would throw in other kinds of food, often oranges or plums, to make up the difference. That's a much more practical and fiscally sound idea than minting small coins that cost more than their value to make, the way we do with pennies and nickels.

Tuk Tuk, 2010
Watercolor, 7" x 9"

I rarely saw these motorized rickshaws being used. Everyone was fit and trim from all the walking. Also, bread and sweets are not common staples. The drivers slept and smoked, reclining in the shade with their helmets on. Gao Ling and I shared a tuk tuk with three teenagers to Leng Shui Jian Mountain, so we could hike to the Buddhist temple on top.

Old Kiln, 2010
Watercolor, 8.5" x 12"

Danny Gregory saw my China drawings on flickr.com and asked for photographs of me drawing for his book, **An Illustrated Journey.** *I was tutoring a young woman named Amber, helping her prepare for the Chinese English Test, a post-college exam. She offered to take the photos while I drew this retired old kiln at the West Virginian Exchange Student building. Amber's brother, a policeman, took us out to dinner. At a karaoke club, Amber's younger sister taught me a dice game I barely understood and couldn't win. She drank me under the table as I belted out pop songs that were way beyond my vocal range or ability, but after untold shots of Baijiu, I didn't care.*

After installing the software that let me illegally access my blog, I found a local copy shop that would scan my drawings for 1 yuan each (about 15¢), and I posted them on-line for friends and family. One day I received an email from Danny Gregory who had seen my drawings on flickr.com. He invited me to write a chapter for his upcoming book *An Illustrated Journey*. Danny's inspirational books on journaling, such as *Everyday Matters, The Creative License,* and especially *An Illustrated Life*, played no small part in motivating me to go to China.

Technically, I had come to teach English, but my real motivation was to draw. That I had come to record my experiences gave me a bird's-eye view objectivity, as if I were a character in a book. Whether my experiences were positive, such as the warm hospitality and sincerity of my students, or the nerve-wracking air and noise pollution of the city, I wanted to record it all faithfully, neither white-washing my loneliness and frustration, nor over-exaggerating the exotic differences. I was determined that whatever happened to me—getting lost or sick, social misunderstandings, having a romantic affair— would all be fodder for a memoir I would eventually write.

Gao Ling suggested I draw her friend's studio. Rainbow lived with a roommate in a tiny third-floor apartment that doubled as a pottery studio.

A plain white room with a sink served as Rainbow's kitchen. Her only appliance was a hotplate that rested on an inverted apple crate on the floor. While I drew the plaster molds (below), the girls chatted in Mandarin, and Rainbow cooked a meal for the four of us. Gao Ling occasionally translated for me, but I was content to listen to their melodic conversation as background music. Though it was cold, the windows were left open for ventilation, and I could see my breath. I was glad to be wearing a heavy leather jacket and thankful I'd had the forethought to bring with me from the U.S. my drawing gloves with the fingertips cut off so I could draw in relative comfort.

When Rainbow called us into the kitchen, I was surprised by the meal she'd been able to make: scrambled eggs and tomatoes, stir-fried green peppers, carrots and cucumbers, juicy and boneless teriyaki chicken, bowls of rice, and I can't remember what else. It was the best meal I'd had in five months. She even had napkins.

I mentioned a card game I'd seen played on the streets, and the girls agreed to teach it to me. It was called *Dou Dizhu*, "Fight the Landlord." Rainbow was a pretty girl who was patient with my efforts to learn the subtleties of the game, and she laughed at my attempts to speak Chinese. She gave me a ceramic Cupid she'd made (see page 131). I was happy with my drawing, and to thank Rainbow for her hospitality, I had a print made of it for her.

Rainbow's Studio, 2010
Watercolor, 8.5" x 12"

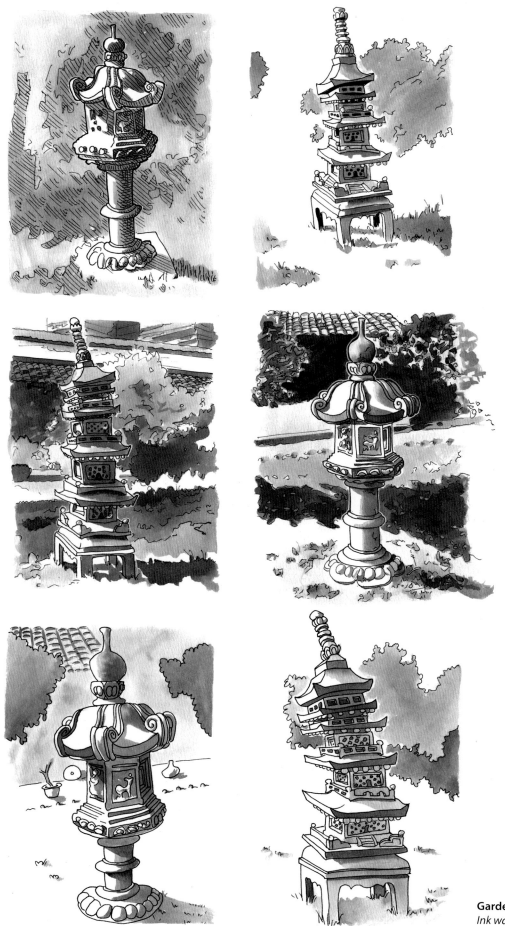

Garden Pagodas, 2010
Ink wash, 14" x 7"

Ingeborg's Bike, 2010
Watercolor, 8.5" x 12"

Inge was a tall, beautiful Norwegian who stayed briefly in the dorm across the hall from me. Gao Ling rushed to introduce us hoping there'd be chemistry. Alas, Inge had a handsome French boyfriend. Besides, she grew tired of my complaining about the pollution and flagrant disregard for traffic safety.

    This is her bike. Notice the industrial kick-stand. Back in Seattle, it was a challenge to find a shop that would even sell me a kickstand, let alone install it. They said it "just wasn't cool."

Toy Vendor, 2011
Watercolor, 8.5" x 12"

At night the sidewalks were covered in blankets and folding tables where people spread out their wares: cellphone covers, shoes, glowing electric clocks, and night-lights. After purging myself of my possessions, I was wary of acquiring anything, but I returned several times to a table full of Mao Zedong's "little red books". They were smaller than I'd imagined, about the size of a full wallet. I was tempted to buy one but refrained. Besides, "Property is theft!"

Sketching Table, 2010
Watercolor, 8.5" x 12"

Gao Ling and her friend "Fish" joined me for a sketch outing. I finished drawing the Pottery Studio (page 117) before they finished their drawings, so I used the time to sketch the table where we had spread our clutter. You can see all three of our phones. I'd meant to save the text messages I received from my Chinese students while in Jingdezhen. Out of the blue, I'd get greetings, well-wishes, and funny non sequiturs. But when I came home, the phone's data wasn't accessible.

Jingdezhen

I studied Mandarin for several months before moving to China and thought I was doing well with it. My background in music and theater helped me to hear and recreate the different tones of Mandarin. In tonal languages, *how* you say a word changes the *meaning* of the word. For example, when the Chinese word "ma" is pronounced in a way that sounds, to Western ears, like a question: "Ma?" it means "hemp." But if you pronounce it like you're trying to get your mother's attention for the umpteenth time, "Ma!" it means "scold." And there are four different tones, so the same verbal unit can mean four different things depending on how you say it. If you use the wrong tone, native Mandarin speakers will not assume which tone you meant to use. In English if you say, "I'd like a hamBURger," emphasizing the second syllable, the waiter will know you want a beef patty between buns. But a similar mistake in China will earn you only a blank stare or worse, you might have said something offensive. For example, the word "wèn," pronounced with a falling tone, means "ask." But "wěn," pronounced with a very low, dipping tone, means "kiss." "Excuse me, may I ask you…?" becomes, "Excuse me, may I kiss you…?" Asking a stranger for directions with the wrong tone is not advised.

To complicate things further, many common Mandarin words have *dozens* of homophones. The word "shi," for example, has over 200 meanings! An entire poem called Shī Shì Shí Shī Shi, "The Story of Shi Eating Lions," is a 92-character poem by Yuen Ren Chao (1892–1982), in which every syllable has the sound "shi" but spoken with different tones.

But these challenges were not my only struggle with Mandarin. Another problem was in hearing the differences between similar consonant sounds. *Shu, chi, sui, si, she, sha, shy, see, shui,* and *sai* all sounded similar to me, and because I couldn't hear the difference, I couldn't pronounce them correctly. This was less important than using the right tones, however, and meant only that I spoke with a very heavy Western accent.

I found reading and writing the characters more fun and interesting. Although the symbols have morphed away from the original pictographs that once made their meanings easy to decode, I was able to create my own graphic mnemonic associations. I saw each character as a little cartoon. Just as English words are made of repeating letters, Chinese characters use "radicals," recurring symbols for water, home, big, and door, for examples. I was often able to get the gist of a new word by looking at the parts I recognized and then considering the context. Using the ATM at the bank wasn't a problem because I knew the radicals for "exit," "left," "right," and "stop," and I knew numbers into the thousands.

My official title, bestowed on me by the Chinese government in order to gain entry, was "Foreign Expert in Oral English." My efforts to learn more Chinese were discouraged by impatient students and vendors who had little interest in helping me figure out how to ask for help. They were eager to learn English and wanted to get on with the transaction at hand. Had I known how unnecessary knowing the language would be, I might have spent less time studying flash cards and listening to audio tapes, and more time studying the history, culture, and customs of China. It became more valuable to master what I came to think of as "Special English." I learned to speak slowly, in stunted phrases filled with pauses and single-syllable words, and to watch closely for signs of confusion. During my first class, a student wrote to me,

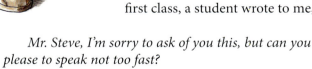

Mr. Steve, I'm sorry to ask of you this, but can you please to speak not too fast?

That evening, Ric asked me, "How was… your… first day of… teaching? Were… your students… happy… to meet you?"

I laughed and said, "Ric, it's me."

He apologized and said it was how he spoke now. I was afraid of sounding condescending to my students, but I copied Ric's example. After my second day of teaching, the same student wrote,

Mr. Steve-
What a good job you have done! I can hear you clearly now. Thank you for your changes in class.

Olga's Place, 2010
Ink wash, 8.5" x 12"

Olga was a Spanish woman studying calligraphy at the Institute. She lived with her Chinese boyfriend off-campus in an apartment with modern conveniences including the only Western-style toilet I saw in Jingdezhen. She said she needed her oasis in the city to maintain her identity and sense of self. The culture of placid stoicism was getting to her. She was afraid of acquiring the same, unemotional, conformist demeanor of the locals.

I saw it myself: pedestrians hit by vehicles got up and walked on without reacting. Stoned-faced shoppers elbowed their way ahead of others without reprisal. Hungry, unkempt cats were tied to doorknobs by strings too short for them to be able to stand on all fours. I walked past a gunny sack, writhing with the bodies of a dozen live ducks. Traffic lights were ignored. Garbage piled up on sidewalks and in rivers where women washed clothes and scrubbed dishes. An infant was run over by a van and when the driver realized what he'd done, he backed over it again to avoid the hospital bills. If he were caught, a funeral was less expensive. Eighteen pedestrians were videotaped by security cameras stepping over or around the baby's pulsing body. A man attempted to help an elderly woman who had been knocked down by a closing bus door, only to find himself responsible for her medical bills because it was decided that only someone responsible for the trouble would stop to help a stranger. When I expressed my concerns in class, a student explained, "This is China."

Ghost Village, 2010
Watercolor, 8.5" x 12"

Alley, 2010
*Watercolor, 8.5" x 12"
(Opposite)*

This drawing became the poster advertising my Friday night lecture at the The Pottery Workshop. Since I don't plan my drawings or use a pencil to place guidelines, sometimes I'm too far into the inking to adjust for errors in proportion. I started drawing the staircase at the top, working my way down, and realized too late that the stairs would not end where they should. That's the way it goes sometimes.

On the long walk to San Bao, I found an abandoned housing development. Acres of three-story brick buildings, with irregularly sized doors and tiny rooms carpeted with rat turds and dead bats. In the U.S. you'd find beer bottles, fire pits, and condoms, but these crumbling buildings were ignored even by kids and the homeless. There was no graffiti or evidence of teens or squatters. I heard different explanations each time I asked: the houses were for sale as they stood, or the project was in limbo. Gao Ling wouldn't discuss it. I was told the story, finally, though I didn't understand the specifics. The developer was an idealistic dreamer who envisioned an American-style suburb, nestled in this verdant valley between San Bao and Jingdezhen. He was either swindled by investors, the government taxed him beyond his ability to recoup, or there was simply no consumer interest in living so far from town. The developer suffered *shī miàn,* "loss of face," and killed himself.

I walked across the road and let myself into the office showroom. Inside was an elaborate and beautifully detailed model of the finished complex, complete with miniature trees and gardens and blue-tiled canals flowing between hundreds of scale buildings. Some of the houses had been jostled off their foundations or lay on their sides, but everything was still there. Nobody had even bothered to lock the showroom door.

Winter Wardrobe, 2010
Watercolor, 8.5" x 12"

The temperature ranged from the muggy nineties when I arrived, to near zero in the winter. I taught classes on Christmas. I was more than twice as old as everyone I knew. I grew tired of being a novelty. I withdrew. I wrote in my journal. I streamed television shows on my laptop. I sketched my room (page 130) and my clothes (above). I was taller and paler than everyone and my clothing drew attention as well. Students asked about my leather jacket and stocking cap. They commented on my fingerless gloves and satchel. When I needed size 12 shoes, Gao Ling took me to every store in the city, but no one sold shoes larger than size 10. Finally, I had my mother send me shoes from the States.

I met two students for lunch, and they were embarrassed by my clothes. The local style was a sport coat over t-shirts or polo-style short sleeves. There was an audible gasp when I removed my jacket and they saw the thermal long sleeves extending from inside my baggy t-shirt. "Seattle-style," I said.

"Hm," they muttered, nodding, "Seattoh stire."

Junk Drawer Stuff, 2010
Watercolor, 12" x 8.5"
(Opposite)

My earplugs for riding the bus, a book light for when the power went off, lunch tokens for the school cafeteria. I must have been complaining more than I realized because my mother sent me the harmonica in a care package. Funny lady.

Nest, 2010
Watercolor, 8.5" x 12"

I'd brought with me from the States an expensive projector that filled half a suitcase. Though I brought only two pieces of luggage for the year, I had prepared animated presentations and slide shows and video clips that I wanted to use in my lessons. I imagined it would be helpful for my students if I were able to use multimedia, as I did in my classroom in Seattle.

On the first day, I packed the projector, some external speakers, journals for the students, chalk (I had to supply my own) and some hand-outs and wheeled it to the bus stop in my carry-on bag. Classes were held on the newer campus, a thirty-minute bus ride from my dorm. Students asked why I was pulling my suitcase around in the 100-degree heat. Other instructors riding the bus whispered and stared.

Sweating, I hauled the suitcase up seven flights of stairs to my class to find that the windows had no curtains, and the sun shown brightly into the room. The projected image was invisible. There was no air-conditioning, and the ceiling fans and open windows drowned out the audio. From then on, I left the projector in my room as a home theater. I watched streaming episodes of *Louis CK* and *Curb Your Enthusiasm*, projected large onto my bare wall.

While judging a drama competition, my sore throat gave out, and I lost my voice completely. That night, in the cone of light coming from the projector, I could see the air was thick with drifting particulates that I'd been inhaling for months. I'd had enough. I felt weak and dizzy. I'd sketched everything in my neighborhood. I was lonely. It was time to go.

I wouldn't leave the students without a teacher for Spring, though. A visiting sculptor and English major had heard my Friday night lecture and asked about my teaching position. I said he could take my place if he wanted it, and he did. I paid a hefty fine for breaking my contract. Students came to my dorm to say goodbye. They brought gifts and asked me to write.

Gao Ling rode in the taxi with me to the airport. I offered to buy her breakfast, but she said she didn't feel well. As we pulled into the terminal, she threw up on the floor of the cab.

Goodbye Gifts, 2010
Watercolor, 8.5" x 12"

Jingdezhen

Greenlake United Methodist Church, 2011
Watercolor, 8.5" x 11"

LOCATION SKETCHING

We all have 10,000 bad drawings in us. The sooner we get them out the better.
        -Walt Stanchfield

Gabriel Campanario, artist and reporter for the **Seattle Times**, began drawing on location as a way to learn about the people and places of his new city when he relocated here from Spain. Gabi is a friendly and prolific illustrator who, in addition to his full-time gig with Seattle's only major newspaper, publishes books on sketching, teaches workshops, gives talks, and manages to hold yearly, sold-out symposiums for urban sketchers around the world. Gabi has been inspiring artists everywhere to come out from behind their desks and immerse themselves in the world around them.

Urban Sketchers grew out of Gabi's drawing group on the photo-sharing website Flickr.com. To be considered an Urban Sketcher, an artist follows a simple manifesto that includes "drawing on location, indoors or out, capturing what we see from direct observation." With an eye toward my next drawing, I began to take more interest in the details of my city and places I visited. Now it's become a habit. I don't walk through a neighborhood or view an urban landscape without at least considering how I would record it.

Edmonds Phone Booth, 2013
Watercolor, 12" x 9"
(Opposite)

Plaster Busts, 2010
Ink wash 8.5" x 11"

I'd been taking night classes at Gage Academy for years. The school holds a yearly Drawing Jam to raise operating funds and scholarships. For the Drawing Jam, the building opens early in the morning and hosts a variety of events. Art supplies are given away, the classrooms are filled with costumed and nude models, musicians, dancers, and faculty demonstrations, crafts rooms are set up for the kids, lunch is available, and student artwork is displayed in the galleries.

I was sketching these busts when I noticed a woman sketching me. It was Gail Wong, an active member of the Seattle Urban Sketchers. We exchanged info, and I joined them for my first time on the next urban sketchcrawl.

Gage Still Life, 2012
Ink wash, 8.5" x 11"

Jack Block Park, 2012
Watercolor and pencil, 11" x 8.5"

Experience Music Project, 2012
Watercolor, 8.5" x 11"

Columbia City Sketchcrawl, 2012
Ink wash, 8.5" x 11"

Urban Sketching   135

Urban Sketchers meet every month or so, usually on a Saturday morning, at a predetermined location. After quick introductions for any new participants, we split off to find our own subjects to draw for the morning. Some go solo while others sit in groups of two or three. At lunch we meet up and spread our sketches out for a sort of show-and-tell before going home to post them on the Urban Sketchers website or on Flickr.

Twice the Seattle Urban Sketchers have gathered to draw near **St. Spiridon Cathedral**. The first time, artist Tommy Kane was visiting from New York and he joined us for the day. I discovered Tommy's work while browsing The Elliott Bay Bookstore with a girlfriend. She called me over to the *Staff Recommendations* shelf. "I think this might interest you," she said, and handed me Danny Gregory's *An Illustrated Life*, a collection of pages from the sketchbooks and private journals of fifty different artists. She was right. I loved this peek into the journals of painters, illustrators, architects, and designers. Although I'd been faithfully journaling and sketching for decades, discovering a culture of like-minded artists renewed and focused my enthusiasm for it.

A few years later, the Seattle Urban Sketchers met again in the same neighborhood. I drew **St. Spiridon Cathedral Again** (opposite) from the exact same location as before to see how my new drawing might differ from the first one.

St. Spiridon Cathedral, 2010
Watercolor, 8.5" x 11"

St. Spiridon Cathedral Again, 2013
Watercolor, 11" x 9"

Urban Sketching

Psychic Energy, 2009
Watercolor, 8" x 11"

My friend Jackie and I met many times to draw different parts of Seattle. We sat in a greasy-spoon diner across from this psychic's shop. Halfway into the drawing, a truck parked outside our window so we had to move, which threw off the perspective a little.

BNSF, 2009
Watercolor, 8.5" x 11"

This drawing was unusual in that I drew it with a brush pen. The only other drawing in this book done with a brush pen is **Plugged-In Teen** *(page 54)*. It looks pretty good, I think. I don't know why I don't use the brush pen more.

Ballard, 2013
Ink wash, 8.5" x 11"

This Ballard park on the intersection of Market and 22nd Ave has a variety of qualities that make it a good subject for sketching: public art, outdoor seating, nearby coffee shops, and restaurants. Four different people sat beside me to talk while I did this drawing, including a retired Hollywood make-up artist.

Chinatown, 2010
Watercolor, 8" x 11"

When Jackie had a professional conference in Canada, I tagged along. While Jackie met with her colleagues, I explored Vancouver with my sketchbook and bought a pair of boots just like hers (see page 145). I drew this view through the window of a café.

Train to Vancouver, 2010
Watercolor, 8" x 11"

The 150-mile train ride from Seattle to Vancouver was a fast, no-stress way to travel. On the nearly empty train, we read, ate, chatted, and sketched each other sketching each other. If you haven't traveled by train, I recommend it.

Four Seasons View, 2010
Watercolor, 8" x 11"

When it was time to check out of our hotel, I was the first one packed. Instead of impatiently tapping my foot or drumming my fingers, I pulled a chair up to the window and drew the view while Jackie and her daughter finished packing in peace.

Urban Sketching

Dentist, 2013
Ink wash, 9" x 11"

Jiffy Lube, 2009
Ink wash, 6" x 9"

Jiffy Lube Again, 2013
Watercolor, 8.5" x 11"

This man was holding a book for a toddler, but they left before I could draw the kid. I'm content to wait, but my subjects often aren't.

Waiting In My Car, 2010
Watercolor, 8.5" x 11"

Have I mentioned I'm always early? Here I am sitting outside Jackie's house, waiting for her to finish who knows what before we go who knows where. Take your time, Lady, I've got a drawing to finish. Relationship counselors should teach sketchbook journaling as a peace-keeping strategy.

Cascade Vista Rehab Center, 2009
Watercolor, 8.5" x 11"

Jackie's dad was recovering from surgery. I'd gone in with her to say hello but came out to the parking lot to give them some time alone and I drew this while I waited.

Shell Oil Demolition, 2009
Watercolor, 8.5" x 11"

Sometimes I'd do a single seven-mile lap around Lake Union and then wait while Jackie ran a second lap. She would often run longer than I could. I set up my stool on the sidewalk and captured this old building midway through being demolished.

Cameron Catering, 2013
Ink wash, 12" x 16"

    The owner of this catering company had a son in my fourth-grade class the first year I taught in 1998. Suzanne is an artist and worked with my students as a guest art teacher. She and her husband Chris were involved parents at Lawton Elementary, chaperoning the week-long outdoor camp, helping to fund and rebuild the playground structures, and catering the school auctions. Cooking was her passion, and she eventually opened her own catering business. Fifteen years after I first met her, I asked Suzanne if I could sit and draw the new company kitchen.

    I was contemplating leaving teaching to pursue art-making so I asked her how it felt, getting to pursue her love of cooking full-time, with a dedicated staff, commercial space, and regular clientele. She said the "business of running the business" was so time-consuming that she had little time for the actual cooking. I made a mental note that if I quit teaching to pursue art-making full-time, not to let the business of art distract me from the joy of drawing.

Vio's, 2013
Watercolor, 8" x 12"

It's nice to have a friend who doesn't mind spending an hour or more over a meal or coffee, contentedly working across the table from me while I draw. I get along best with busy people with work they can do on a laptop or iPad while I sketch the surroundings. Jackie and I spent many evenings in restaurants and coffee shops while she worked on a book that was due to the publisher or graded her students' essays. Sitting in silence is my idea of a good time. I'm the life of the party.

Vio's Kitchen, 2013
Ink wash, 12" x 8"

Jackie's Dining Room, 2010
Ink wash, 8.5" x 11"

Jackie's Living Room, 2010
Ink wash, 8.5" x 11"

Jackie at Work, 2010
Ink wash, 8.5" x 11"

In addition to authoring several academic textbooks on criminal psychopathy, serving as the chair of the Criminal Justice Department at Seattle University, and regularly drawing with the Urban Sketchers, Jackie is also a Marathon Maniac, a title bestowed on runners who complete at least three full marathons (26.2 miles each) within 90 days. Jackie was one of the unlucky runners who flew to New York for the marathon only to find it canceled due to Superstorm Sandy. Here she is working in her office.

Jackie's Boots, 2009
Ink wash, 8.5" x 11"

Urban Sketching

Sebi's Polish Bistro, 2012
Watercolor, 12" x 8.5"

Lighthouse, 2010
Watercolor, 8.5" x 11"

Discovery Park Lighthouse, 2012
Watercolor, 8.5" x 11"

Urban Sketching   147

Georgetown Bar, 2010
Ink wash, 9" x 11"

Smash Wine Bar, 2013
Ink wash, 9" x 11"

Zoka's Coffee, 2010
Ink wash, 11" x 9"

Suzallo Library, 2009
Uni-Ball pen, 8.5" x 11"

Some Urban Sketchers experiment with inks and different pen nibs. They build custom, portable travel kits out of Altoid tins and film canisters. They chat about technical pens, brands of watercolor, and the advantages of different weights of paper.

As for me, I draw with Uni-ball pens I buy in bulk at Staples. I've used the same brushes for years. I don't mean the brand; I mean the same four or five white, sable brushes have traveled to China, Bangkok, Singapore, Mexico, and through fifteen different states. I buy the same Canson all-purpose sketchbooks every time. Maybe I should branch out, try some different tools, but when I'm drawing, I just follow the contours of the object I'm drawing, trying to fit the pieces together on the page, squinting to see the darks and lights, and deciding what to include and what to leave out. The issues I mull while drawing would be the same if I were scratching the lines in sand with a stick.

Suzallo Library Interior, 2013
Ink wash, 11" x 8.5"

Women's Correctional Facility, 2013
Ink wash, 8.5" x 11"

I joined Gabi Campanario and about ten other Urban Sketchers for a workshop at the women's prison near Gig Harbor, Washington. We hoped to offer a fun and open-ended visual activity to compliment the IF Project, where inmates write personal responses to the question, "If there was something someone could have said or done that would have changed the path that led you here, what would it have been?"

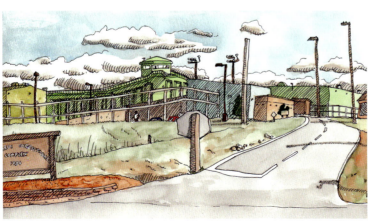

Monroe Prison, 2010
Watercolor, 7" x 11"

I was invited to join a small group of educators for an evening with the "lifers" (violent offenders who were sentenced to life behind bars) at Monroe Prison. After a thorough prescreening and vetting process we went inside and sat in a large circle to hear the stories, often sad and moving, of men struggling with histories I could barely imagine. I drew these views of the facility before going inside.

Belltown, *2012*
Watercolor, 9" x 11"

Ballard, *2012*
Watercolor, 9" x 11"

Orient Express, 2010
Watercolor, 9" x 11"

Vine Street Storage, 2013
Watercolor, 9" x 11"

Urban Sketching

Bedlam Coffee, *2009*
Uni-Ball pen, 8" x 11"

Donna at Bedlam Coffee, *2013*
Ink wash, 8.5" x 11"

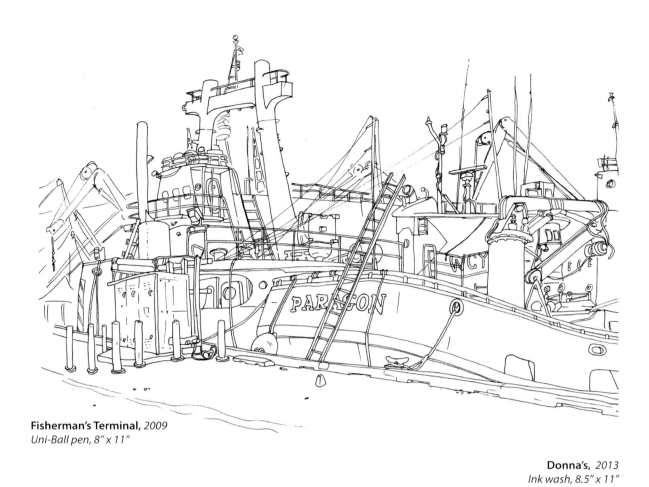

Fisherman's Terminal, *2009*
Uni-Ball pen, 8" x 11"

Donna's, *2013*
Ink wash, 8.5" x 11"

Urban Sketching

Shilshole House, 2009
Ink wash, 9" x 8"

The tenant of this strange house near Shilshole Marina came out to chat with me while I drew. He was renting from the man who lived in the house that can be seen to the left in the drawing. The owner built the place to look like a lighthouse, obviously, but the current renter said that as a residence it was not very practical. The tower is barely large enough to stand in, and the rest of the house is not much bigger. The location, right across the street from the marina was nice, he said, and it worked well enough as a temporary bachelor pad for a young, single man.

Eastlake Bridge, 2009
Ink wash, 8" x 11"

Georgetown Trucks, *2009*
Ink wash, 8" x 11"

Georgetown Truck, *2009*
Watercolor, 8" x 11"

Urban Sketching   157

Serendipity, 2012
Ink wash, 3.5" x 11"

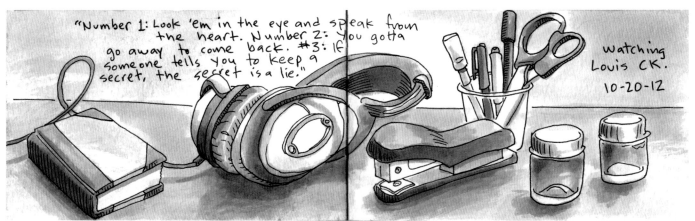

Watching Louis CK, 2012
Ink wash, 3.5" x 11"

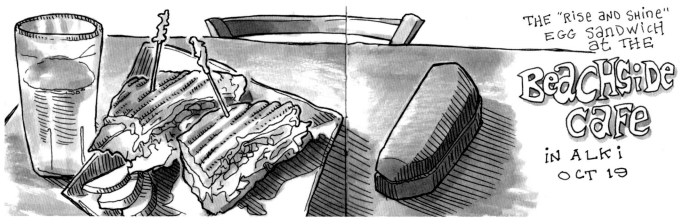

Beachside Café, 2012
Ink wash, 3.5" x 11"

Market Avenue, 2012
Ink wash, 3.5" x 11"

Magnolia, 2012
Ink wash, 3.5" x 11"

Greenlake Rain, 2012
Ink wash, 3.5" x 11"

BANGKOK

Twenty years from now you will be more disappointed by the things you didn't do than by the ones you did do.
   -Mark Twain

Through posting drawings to the Urban Sketchers website, I had come to know, at least virtually, some of the sketchers in Bangkok. On my way home from Jingdezhen, I decided to take advantage of my proximity to other places I wanted to see and caught a flight from Jingdezhen to Thailand. After a few days of exploring and sketching on my own, Asnee Tasna, a prolific sketcher, instructor, and all-around nice guy, helped organize an ad hoc day of sketching the historic sites of Bangkok, beginning with Wat Phra Kaew, Temple of Emerald Buddha. There was so much to see that I was restless and impatient. I couldn't stay put and my sketches were not very good. After a few hours of struggling on my own, we met for lunch and passed our books around. I drew the **Guardian** (below) in the humid tropical sun. After some more sketching, I took a boat ride on the Chao Phraya River back to my tiny but very comfortable room overlooking the narrow streets of the Phranakorn section of Bangkok.

Plane to Bangkok, 2011
Watercolor, 8.5" x 12"

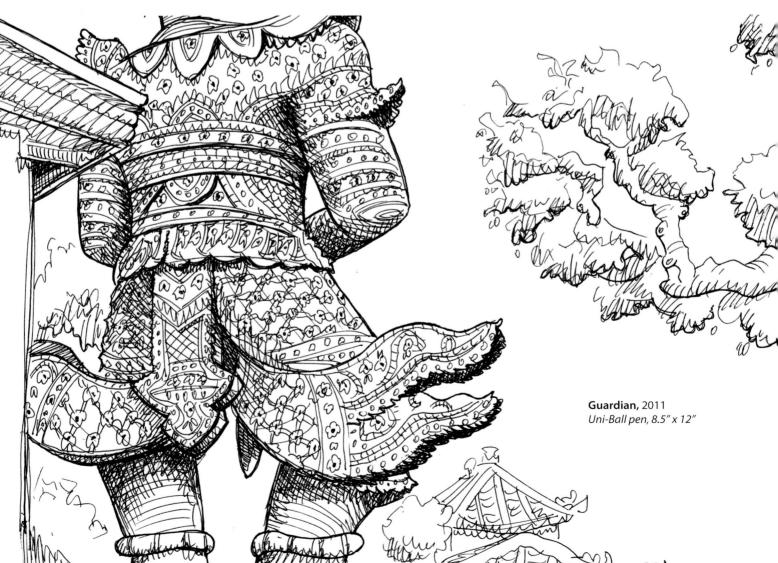

Guardian, 2011
Uni-Ball pen, 8.5" x 12"

Urban Bangkok, 2011
Watercolor, 12" x 8.5"

Bangkok

Bangkok Home, 2011
Watercolor, 7" x 9"

More than the guided tour, I enjoyed my leisurely strolls through the non-touristy neighborhoods, mingling with locals, losing myself in the strange and unfamiliar. Olga, the Spanish student in China, had suggested the hotel. It was clean, quiet, had free wi-fi, complimentary breakfast, A/C, and a little balcony from which to watch the locals going about their business. I won't tell you where I stayed. As the song goes, "Call some place paradise, and kiss it goodbye."

Wat, 2011
Watercolor, 12" x 8.5"

At my hostel, I signed up for an all-day tour and saw so many temples, wats, and religious sites in such a short time that they began to blend together. There wasn't enough time at each site to do very detailed drawings, but I met some interesting free souls on the trip and took a lot of notes and photos.

Green Café, 2011
Ink wash, 12" x 8.5"

Gage Life Session 2013
Watercolor, 9" x 12"

DRAWING PEOPLE

A lot of what I do is just the mental illness of persistence.
　　-Nicholson Baker

If you can draw the figure, you can draw anything, or so the thinking goes. We know immediately when a drawing of a person is "off." We are expertly familiar with our own bodies, and, one assumes, with a few others. It's harder for an artist to get away with distorting humans than, say, trees, because we're instinctive judges of the appearance of humans. I rarely include people in my sketches because I draw slowly, and people don't tend to hold still unless they're paid to. However, the hours I spend working from models are probably the most beneficial use of my drawing time.

　　I continue to take classes today for the same reason I've always taken classes: I like to learn, and I learn best by doing things that are hard for me. I like the structure and deadlines of a formal class. I like the camaraderie of artists, discussing the challenges and rewards of a life of art, and watching artists during the process of making art. With luck there'll be someone in the class with skills that blow me away. I'll see their photo-realistic work and think, "Wow," though it's not my goal to draw like that. I don't have the patience, first of all. And maybe not the talent, if you believe in that sort of thing. The idea of talent is sort of insulting, really. Isn't talent just dedication and practice? "Talent" is a concept we use to excuse ourselves for not working harder.

Aaron, 2013
Watercolor, 9" x 12"

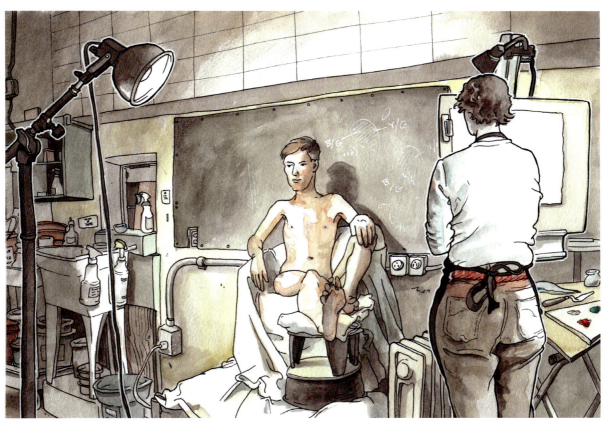

Christopher, 2013
Watercolor, 9" x 12"

Drawing People

Gage #1, 2013
Ink wash, 11" x 14"

Several times a week, the Gage Academy offers drop-in figure sessions. I hadn't drawn from the figure for years, focusing instead on quick outdoor captures and drawings of cluttered vintage shops. I decided I could use the practice. This drawing was from my first time back in the studio after many years. When I sat to draw the model, I took in the whole room and drew everything I could see just as I had been drawing outdoors. I had to work fast, which helped reduce any fussiness, and it's one of the few instances where people held still long enough for me to include them.

The college classes I remember as the most practical—courses in which I got the biggest bang for my buck—were the Anatomy for Artists classes taught by Paul Buckner at the University of Oregon in the mid-eighties. Paul knew his subject. He broke down the structures of the human body in ways that made engineering sense. He walked the walk, pointing to specific features on the model and sketching examples on the chalkboard, clearly diagramming how the underlying bone and muscle affected the surface anatomy we were attempting to draw.

It's a small world. Thirty years later Paul Buckner's son Matt now teaches Figure Drawing and Anatomy at the Gage Academy here in Seattle.

Kneeling Gesture, 2001
Charcoal, 24" x 18"

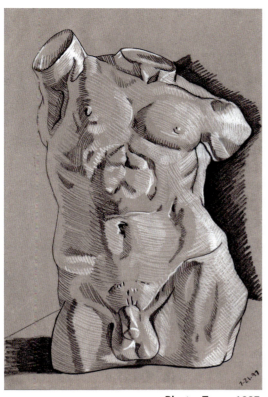

Plaster Torso, 1997
Conté Crayon, 24" x 18"

Back, 1997
Conté Crayon, 24" x 18"

30-second Gesture, 2001
Charcoal, 12" x 18"

Drawing People

Bowtie, 1998
Pencil, 30" x 24"

Rockwell, 1998
Pencil, 30" x 24"

Throughout college, I was undisciplined and distracted. I spent as much time performing in musical theater as I did drawing. I studied literature, philosophy, and computer science. I thought for a while I would be a filmmaker. I dropped out of school repeatedly: sometimes for work because I had no money, but just as often because I was impatient and romantic. I was reading Kerouac and Bukowski. I was making animated films and learning to play the piano. I twice enrolled in the same graduate level existentialism course, and both times dropped out of school midway through the semester because I worried that "real life" was passing me by while I sat in a dark room in an uncomfortable chair. I moved to San Fransisco. I followed a girlfriend to Fort Collins, Colorado. I went to Alaska to build a haunted house with my brother in Anchorage.

It took me eight years to earn my Bachelor of Fine Arts from the University of Oregon, and even then I had to argue for my degree because my final project was a film and film was part of the School of Communications, not the School of Art. *Didn't you consult with an advisor,* the review board asked, *before spending months on a project that wouldn't qualify as your final project?* No, I said. I had never met with an advisor. Ever. They took another look at my transcripts and saw that I hadn't completed the required Color Theory courses, either. Rolling their eyes, they let me graduate anyway, probably because they were tired of me.

Skull, 1998
Oil, 30" x 24"
(Opposite)

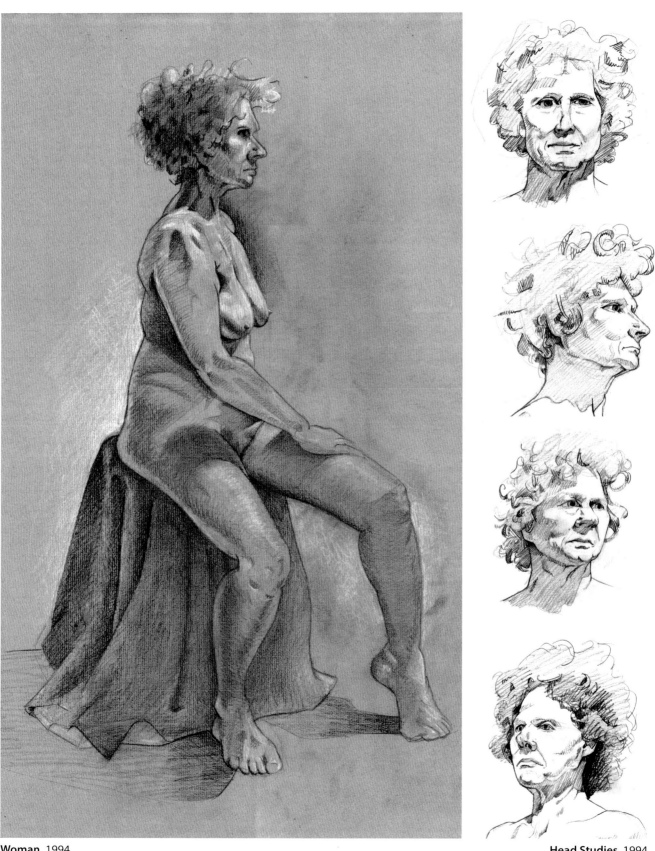

Woman, 1994
Conté Crayon, 30" x 24"

Head Studies, 1994
Graphite

Seated Male, 1991
Pencil, 30" x 24"

Drawing People

Seated female, 1992
Pencil, 24" x 30"

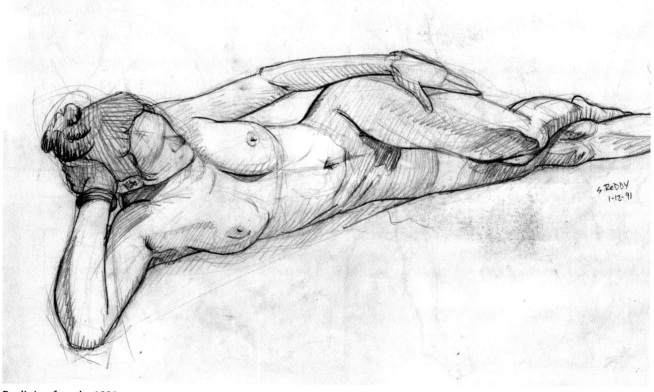

Reclining female, 1991
Pencil, 20" x 30"

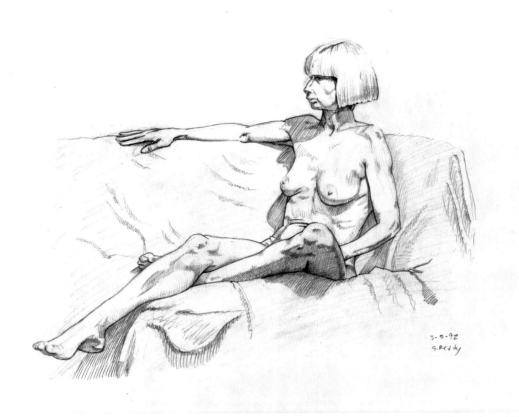

Page, Seated 1, 1992
Pencil, 24" x 30"

Page, Seated 2, 1992
Pencil, 24" x 30"

Drawing People

Seated Male, 2009
Conté Crayon, 30" x 24"

Seated Male, 2009
Charcoal, 30" x 24"

 I've been drawing from models since high school. I was lucky to have a great art teacher at Dimond High School in Anchorage, Alaska. Ric Swenson was a dedicated, easy-going guy we students respected and admired. He had a fully-equipped art room with potter's wheels, a kiln, and all the supplies we needed. The room was always open so we could hang out discussing or making art during lunch or after school.

 One day, when I was a junior, I went home for lunch with Dana, the student who had shown me his private sketchbook journal and inspired my own obsessive chronicling. At his house he gave me a "special" cookie and then drove me back to school. I had art after lunch, and students were taking turns posing for the rest of the class to draw. I stared at my blank paper. Where should I begin? I studied the folds of the boy's shirt, but when I looked to the paper in front of me I saw only the fibrous texture of the newsprint. How could I look at the model and control my drawing hand at the same time? My graphite marks bore no relationship to the boy sitting in the chair way over there by the window. Drawing suddenly seemed insurmountably complicated. The girl across from me began crying. "Look at his eyes!" she sobbed. "Oh my God, he's stoned!" She ran to tell Mr. Swenson who calmly sent a student to find Dana so he could drive me home to sleep it off.

 Thirty-five years later I reconnected with Ric through Facebook, and he offered me the job teaching in China. I asked him about the incident, but, naturally, he had no memory of the wasted kid in his class.

Christine Reading, 2013
Watercolor, 8.5" x 11"

Christine Sleeping, 2013
Watercolor, 8.5" x 11"

Drawing People 177

Guy Pierce, 2013
Uni-ball, 8.5" x 11"

Donna invited me over for dinner. While she cooked, we chatted and I drew her living room (page 155). On another visit, I flipped through the magazines on her coffee table and drew these images from photos. I don't know who Guy Pierce is. He's an actor in a movie, one about fighting, it seems. There's an angry guy with a gun. Is Guy the guy with the gun? Or is Guy the other guy?

Model, 2013
Ink, 11" x 8.5"

Dr. Sketchy's, 2010
Uni-Ball, 9" x 12"

Roller Derby, 2011
Watercolor, 8.5" x 11"

Drawing People

For decades I used cheap, student-grade sketchbooks with thin paper that wrinkled. They were the cheapest books available, and it didn't occur to me that they should last. I filled them quickly. To tell them apart, I made covers for them, the way we were taught in grade school to protect the school's textbooks. I folded covers out of maps, posters, calendars, programs from galleries, and art-house movie schedules. *Winter '81* is covered with a chart from Safeway showing different kinds of red meat. *Winter '82* is covered in a thin blue bandana that my girlfriend wore like a Russian peasant. Not until 2010, when I began regularly using India ink washes and could afford better books, did I switch to spiral-bound watercolor books with 90-lb paper that could hold moisture. I have to take them apart to lay the drawings flat in the scanner, but the paper doesn't wrinkle like these did.

Man, *1992*
Ink wash, 11" x 8.5"

Woman, *1992*
Ink wash, 11" x 8.5"

Homunculus, *1992*
Prismacolor, 11" x 8.5"

Crawling Woman, *1992*
Prismacolor, 11" x 8.5"

Jenga, *1992*
Prismacolor, 11" x 17"

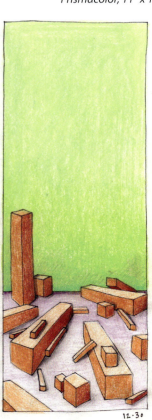

Drawing People

Kissing Potion Study 1, *2009*
Watercolor, 11" x 8.5"

Kissing Potion Study 2, *2009*
Watercolor, 11" x 8.5"

Joy Davenport is the lead singer for the funk-and-soul band, *Kissing Potion*. She gave me the palmwood tikis I gave away (page 91) just before moving to China. If I remember correctly, a bandmate split up with his girlfriend, and he had nowhere to store them except in the band's rehearsal space. Joy had heard from her daughter, who was in my fifth-grade class, that I had a thing for the South Pacific. When the band grew tired of stepping around the tikis, Joy offered them to me. She also asked if I'd make a flyer for an upcoming gig they were sharing with some other Seattle Bands at the Comet Tavern in Seattle. I looked at some pictures of the different bands on-line and doodled around for a while (above). Then I combined some of the doodles I liked best into one image (opposite page). For the final poster, Joy added the text (right).

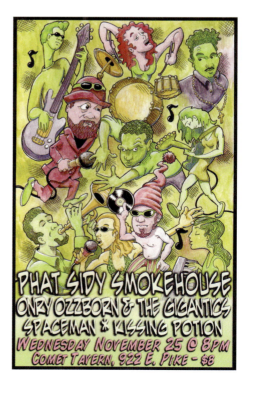

Kissing Potion, 2009
Watercolor, 14" x 11"

KP Apothecary, *2012*
Watercolor, 8" x 8"

A few years after creating the flyer for Kissing Potion's Seattle gig, the band asked if I'd create an image for a new CD they were about to release. I suggested images of bottles and paraphernalia (opposite), but they wanted the band browsing in an apothecary, holding different potions and elixirs. I was in Long Beach visiting my cousins at the time, so I wasn't able to get the band together to pose for photos. Nor did I have any references for an apothecary, so I just made the whole thing up.

KP Bottles, *2012*
Watercolor, 8" x 8"

The images on this page were used on the inside and back of the CD cover. I originally thought the song titles could appear on the labels of the bottles, but either there wasn't time or the final playlist hadn't been set. I don't remember.

KP Lab, *2012*
Watercolor, 8" x 8"

I thought this drawing of science paraphernalia might suggest the kind of things a chemist would use to create potions. It wasn't until after the image was printed that it looked to me like a collection of addictive vices. At a glance, the horizontal test tube resembles a cigarette, the beaker looks like a carafe of red wine, and the four-tiered thing looks like a bong. When I pointed this out to Joy, she said, "All the better."

Drawing People   185

Gage Dancers, 2013
Ink wash, 9" x 12"

Newspaper Ad, 2013
Printed in Seattle's **The Stranger**

I posted some drawings from the Gage figure sessions, and the school contacted me about creating artwork for posters and newspaper ads for an upcoming Drawing Jam (see page 134). The Gage website had archived photos from previous Jams so I browsed through them and selected images that had some characters that I liked: pirates, an earnest-looking artist, a family drawing together. I collaged the people into groups much the same way I did the Kissing Potion flyer (page 182-183), arranging them on tracing paper until they made a somewhat cohesive cluster. I wanted to represent the different aspects of the event so I offered to make three drawings, each with a different focus: music, dance, and costumes. In exchange for the drawings, I asked Gage for a season pass for drop-in figure drawing sessions.

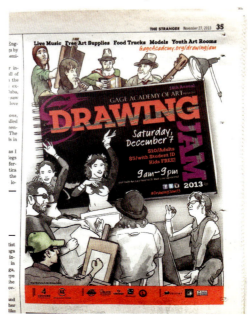

Gage Pirates, 2013
Watercolor, 9" x 12"

Gage Musicians, 2013
Watercolor, 9" x 12"

Drawing People 187

SINGAPORE

Singapore is Disneyland with the death penalty.
    -William Gibson

For two weeks I explored this modern city-state, passing white-tiled restaurants and shops selling Gucci and Versace. It felt more like Boca Raton than Southeast Asia.

The Singapore Sketchers held an ad hoc day of drawing during my visit. I asked where everybody lived because I had sketched all over but had seen no houses. Most Singaporeans, I was told, live in high-rise government housing projects—self-contained vertical towns with schools, supermarkets, clinics, and recreational facilities all contained within the same building.

The Singaporeans I met were understandably proud of their safe and pristine city, which I silently contrasted with the vandalism and violence back home. There was no trash and no graffiti, because they were caning offenses. Being caught chewing gum could cost you $2,000. On arrival, I had been handed an official warning: *Mandatory execution for transportation of drugs.* Singapore has one of the lowest crime rates in the world, but then, they are willing to give up some liberties in exchange. Something to think about.

David Elias Bldg, Selegie Rd, 2011
Watercolor, 8.5" x 12"

Cathedral of the Good Shepard, 2011
Watercolor, 8.5" x 11"

Club Street, 2011
Uni-Ball pen, 11" x 8.5"

Singapore

St. Joseph's Cathedral, 2011
Watercolor, 11" x 8.5"

Raffles Ave Bay View, 2011
India ink, 8.5" x 11"

*The Singapore Urban Sketchers are a group of talented artists led by the cheerful Tia Boon Sim. Tia gave me copies of **Urban Sketchers Singapore, Vol. 1** and Gabi's **The Art of Urban Sketching**, which hadn't yet been released in the US. I enjoyed my dinner in Little India with Ali Sajid, a skilled painter who had recently brought his family from Pakistan. He'd discovered Singapore on his honeymoon three years earlier. Our warm chat over a delicious meal in Little India was a highlight of my visit.*

Masjid Jamae Mosque, 2011
India ink, 8.5" x 11"

ORIGINS

"If others examined themselves attentively, as I do, they would find themselves, as I do, full of inanity and nonsense."

   -Montaigne

The influence of comics and Saturday morning animation on my drawing is pretty obvious. In preschool, I practiced drawing the characters from Pillsbury's Funny Face drink packets: Jolly-Olly Orange, Rootin'-Tootin' Raspberry, Choo-Choo Cherry. Lying on the floor in front of the television, I drew Fred Flintstone and the Looney-Toons gang. I was scolded for tracing the greeting cards my mother bought for others because the pressure of my pencil left grooves in the face of the cards.

In third grade I drew a "stripper machine." A woman entered the drawing from the left and fell down a manhole to land on a conveyor belt which moved her through a series of robotic claws that tore off her clothes. Then she popped back up through another manhole on the right side of the page to continue walking, naked and oddly unperturbed by the experience. The drawings were confiscated when I got caught sketching copies for the other boys in class. Mrs. Anderson was not a fan.

Short Subjects, 1982
Mixed Medic, 11" x 8.5"
(Opposite)

Early Journal/Sketchbook, 1982
Mixed Media, 11" x 17"

Science, 1981
India ink and Prismacolor, 11" x 8.5"

Mouse, 1983
Tech pen and Prismacolor, 6" x 8"

At 15, I won a juried art-competition with a drawing of a six-fingered guitarist. I'd recently bought my first electric six-string with money earned after school cleaning the machines in a meat market. I came up with the idea for the drawing while trying to play a difficult chord.

In high school, my grades suffered. I acted in plays and sang in the jazz choir, but I skipped classes to hang out in the school's theater or in the art room. When I did attend class, I mostly drew pictures or read novels. One day Dana, a senior, saw me drawing and said, "We need an art guy on the yearbook staff." I became the yearbook illustrator. This same student showed me his journal: an 11" x 8.5" hardbound book of drawings, clippings, scripts, notes, and random musings. It felt intimate to me, confessional but without apology. I bought my own sketchbook and started writing and drawing in it. That book, begun on October 2nd, 1978, is pretentious and immature. The drawings are embarrassing. But I kept at it. By spring the book was full, and on June 1st I started another one.

My Pens and Stuff, 1986
Prismacolor, 10" x 8"

It Must Be The Weather, 1987
Prismacolor, 10" x 8"

I have mixed feelings about sharing these old diary-style entries. They're crudely drawn and sometimes intentionally opaque. They're embarrassing the way diaries often are. Looking at them now, I suspect in some cases I was just trying to fill pages, to get on with it. On the other hand, they're still oddly engaging to me, though probably not to anyone else. Much the way dreams are boring to anyone but the dreamer.

Sixty sketchbooks later, I feel like I'm beginning to get the hang of it. I use higher quality spiral-bound watercolor tablets. I don't mess them up with my to-do lists, financial calculations, and fretful, midnight worries. Now if someone asks to see them, I don't have to read over her shoulder, ready to flip quickly past a page of sentimentality, ill-formed fantasies, regrets and obsessions. I have separate, lined notebooks for all that.

Whatever, 1989
India ink, 14" x 11"

196   Now Where Was I?

New Year's Eve, 1991
Prismacolor, 10" x 8"

Death of an Artist, 1991
Prismacolor, 10" x 8"

A Slight Headache, 1991
Prismacolor, 10" x 8"

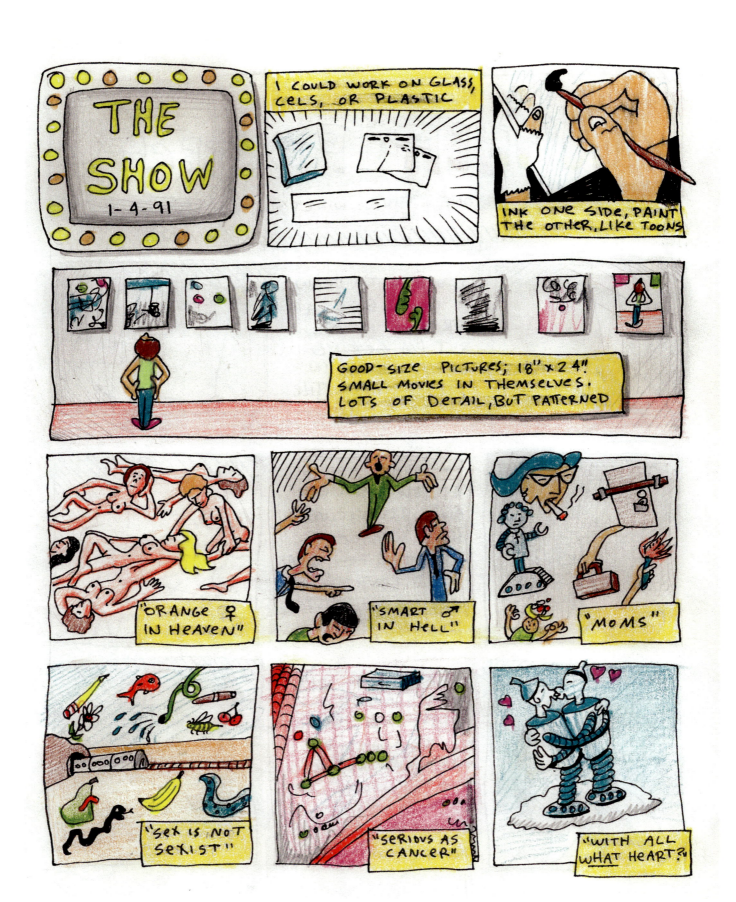

The Show, 1991
Prismacolor, 10" x 8"

Sleepless Nights, 1991
Prismacolor, 10" x 8"

Like a Pendulum, 1991
Prismacolor, 11" x 8"

2:58, 1991
Mixed media, 11" x 8"

Genesis, 1991
India ink, 24" x 18"

Mental Block, 1991
India ink, 24" x 18"

Journal Page, 1991
Prismacolor, 11" x 8"

Wax, 1991
Prismacolor, 11" x 8.5"

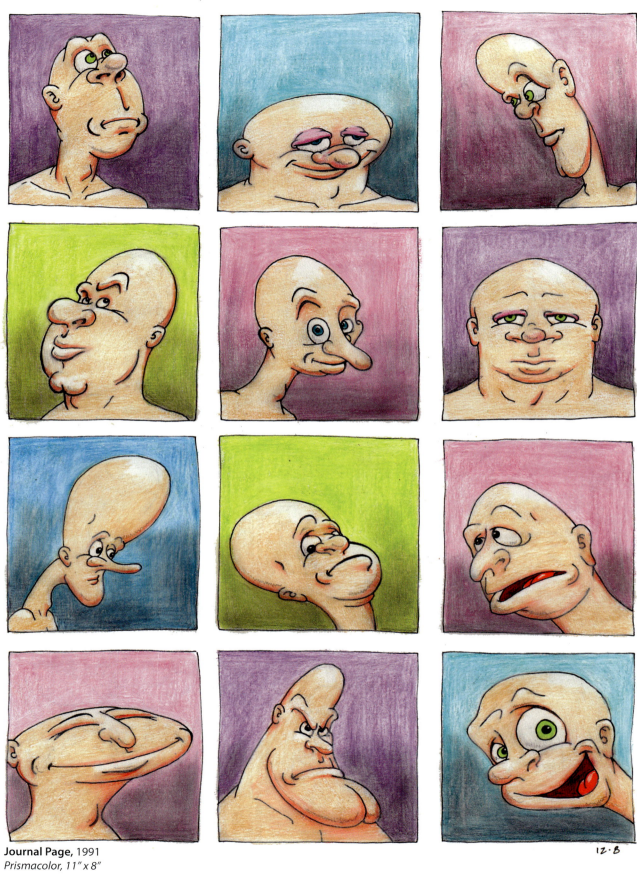

Journal Page, 1991
Prismacolor, 11" x 8"

Journal Page, 1991
Prismacolor, 11" x 8"

Trim, 1991
Prismacolor, 10" x 8"

Doors, 1991
Prismacolor, 8" x 8"

Still Here, 1991
Prismacolor, 11" x 17"
(next spread)

Journal Page, 1991
Prismacolor, 11" x 8.5"

Untitled, 1991
Prismacolor, 11" x 16"

Purple Paisley Page, 1991
Prismacolor, 11" x 16"

Origins

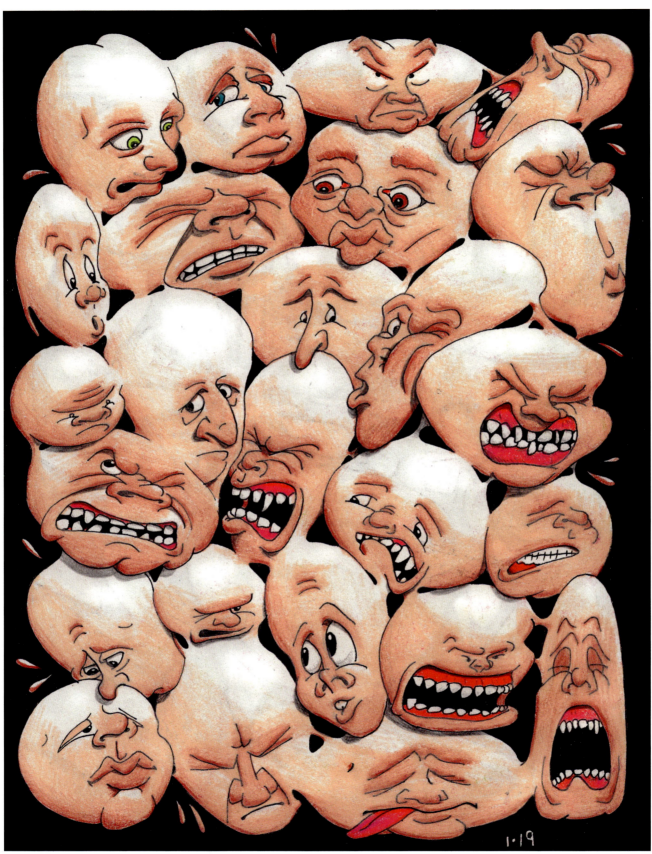

Company, 1991
Prismacolor, 11" x 8.5"

Weyerhaeuser Commission, 1987
India ink, 8.5" x 8"

As kids, my brother Dan and I were allowed to stay up late on Fridays watching *Nightmare Theater Double Feature*. From our sleeping bags on the floor, we watched countless classic horror films and B-movies made in the 50s and 60s. As we got older, we studied magazines like *Fangoria* to learn how to make fake blood with Karo syrup and food-coloring and prosthetic limbs with plaster casts filled with latex and dental alginate. We read up on masters of make-up gore like Tom Savini and Rick Baker. We borrowed our parents' tape-recorder to make radio plays. With their cheap Instamatic cameras we shot slide-show vampire photo-plays.

When I was 24, I dropped out of college to join Dan in Anchorage to build a haunted house. We rented a spot in a strip mall, obtained a business license and insurance, and had radio and newspaper ads made. We borrowed 9K from family and friends with a promise of 10% interest on their investment. We built a plywood maze and made prosthetic limbs we could sever and mutilate while our friends acted like werewolves and mad-scientists. We stayed up all night working in the dark, spooked by our own creations. Then we'd come home and sleep until the afternoon, eat a bowl of Mr. T cereal and head back to work.

After two months of building the sets and leafleting the cars in the high school parking lots, we opened our doors to thousands of bored teens waiting in line outside in the Alaskan cold. We opened a week before Halloween and made enough money opening-night to pay back our investors. The rest of the week was pure profit. And that's how I made enough money to buy my first car, a small Fiat, that I would soon be living in when I returned to college in Eugene, Oregon.

Everything, All The Time, 1991
India ink, 11" x 17"
(next spread)

Origins

ACAPULCO

One travels more usefully when alone, because he reflects more.
   -Thomas Jefferson

The Grand Mayan Resort lies on the beach a few miles south of Acapulco Bay. Drug cartel violence in the city has scared away tourists so luxury rooms can be had cheap. At 40% capacity, the place feels deserted, which is one of the draws for my coming here every year. I don't use the internet. The hotel television stays off. I stay for several weeks at a time, alone, to draw, swim, and read. I walk the beach for miles in either direction. Further south along the beach is Playa Bonfil, with sun-baked Dutch and German tourists playing billiards on an outdoor table, and local surfers showing off for their girlfriends.

I've become friends with a few of the locals. I even recognize individual animals: the bird with the broken foot, the fat iguana, and the giant soggy scarab who dried out while resting in my cap. I've had a look around the cheap apartments and condos, tempted to stay. It's just a fantasy though. I'd miss Seattle's arts-culture and the liberal, progressive scene I've become part of.

During my last visit I overdid the sun and cooked myself pretty badly. Unable to go outside for a week, I drew interiors, such as the *Mayan Palace Lobby* (below).

Acapulco Hillside, 2011
Uni-ball, 12" x 8.5"
(Opposite)

An armed guard said I couldn't draw these houses. "Propiedad privada," he said.

"Por favor, Señor," I showed him my sketchbook. "Con su permision. Solomente una hora. Soy un artiste."

He adjusted his AR15 and looked up at the houses. He held up a finger. "Una hora," he said and sat in the shade of a nearby tree and closed his eyes.

When I finished an hour later, I called out, "Gracias!"

Without opening his eyes he muttered, "De nada."

Mayan Palace Lobby, 2013
Watercolor, 8.5" x 12"

Grand Mayan Lobby, 2009
Uni-Ball pen, 8.5" x 12"

Aca Well, 2011
Watercolor, 8.5" x 12"

Water Park, 2012
Watercolor, 8.5" x 12"

Water Park Hippo, 2012
Watercolor, 8.5" x 12"

I choose a subject for various reasons: Is it visually interesting? Is there a clear foreground, middle ground, and background? Is it something I can commit to staring at for two or more hours? Is there a comfortable place to sit, out of the sun or away from distractions? What will I have to listen to while I draw?

I drew the kids' section of the pool because of the interesting geometry and for the sounds of the water splashing and the wind rustling the palm fronds.

Acapulco

True Story, 2011
Watercolor, 12" x 8.5"

Volkswagons, 2009
Watercolor, 8.5" x 12"

Acapulco is where old VWs go to retire. If you've ever owned a Volkswagon Van or Beetle, it's probably here somewhere.

Aca Beach, 2009
Uni-Ball, 8.5" x 12"

Wading in the shallow surf, with my running shoes in my hand, a vendor caught up and kept pace with me.
  "Hola, Amigo!"
  "¡Buenas!," I said.
  He held up an arm, heavy with shell necklaces.
  "No, gracias," I said, and kept walking.
  "But Señor," he smiled, "Almost free!"
  "Ah," I smiled back. "Then I'll almost buy one."

Acapulco

Acapulco Rat, 2013
Watercolor, 11" x 17"

OIL PAINTING

Painting is easy when you don't know how, but very difficult when you do.

      -Edgar Degas

After three years, my house-flipping project was finished and in the winter there was little to do in Bremerton on the weekends. I was commuting to work all week, so the last thing I wanted to do on my days off was to make another four-hour round-trip to Seattle. I had time and a garage. I decided to teach myself how to paint. I had a B.F.A. in Visual Design, but I'd never painted in oil or acrylics. I knew nothing about mediums, drying time, or brushes. Would I paint on canvas or some kind of board? Where would I pour my spent thinners and medium? I bought a space heater, a large, wooden easel and set to work on a 4' x 3' canvas. Intimidated by the size of the painting, the first thing I did was divide it up into smaller frames. Then I filled each one with color. Afraid to over-think it, I started filling the frames automatically with whatever popped into my head. In a few hours, I had **Rebus #1** (below, left).

Rebus #3, 2007
Oil, 36" x 24"

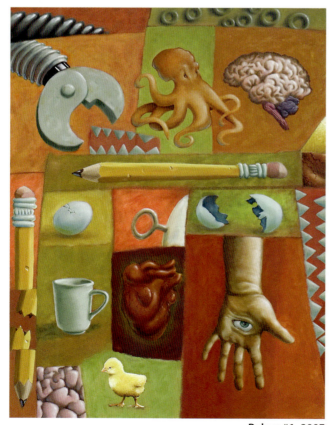

Rebus #1, 2007
Oil, 48" x 36"

Rebus #2, 2007
Oil, 30" x 24"

Rebus #6, 2008
Oil, 30" x 30"

I played my music loud and worked quickly, not knowing what would appear in the paintings until I painted them. I chose objects without thinking, letting juxtaposition and visual properties imply links and relationships. Only when I had a show of a dozen paintings in this series, did I step back and wonder what I'd been doing. I thought maybe the "frames" were born of my interest in comics. Being an elementary school teacher played a part, I'm sure, in the toy-like way I rendered everything. Now, years later, I still enjoy looking at these paintings. It's as if they were done by someone else. I kept a few favorites, but most of them sold.

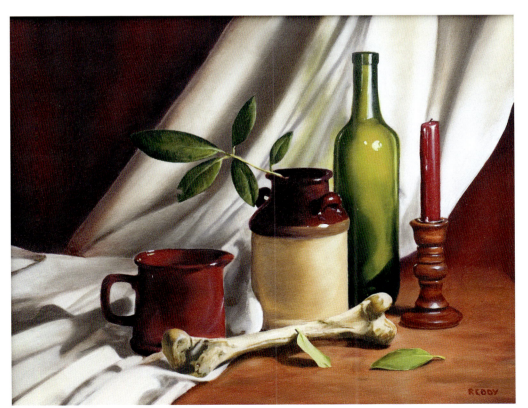

Still-Life, 2007
Oil, 18" x 24"

After messing around on my own for a while, I took a beginning painting workshop at the Gage Academy. I came home and set up my own still life of things from around the house, including a deer femur my son and I found while camping at Green River.

Oil Painting

In my sketchbook I made a list of objects from a typical day: my morning shower, a mocha, the '77 Nova that was my late brother's, a letter to my son, and my garden. The old television is the one I grew up with in the sixties. The bicycle is more iconic than the Trek 7300 I was commuting on each day, but I was more interested in learning how to paint than being biographically faithful. I collaged everything together chronologically, starting in the upper left and reading back and forth like the page of a comic. This time I left out the panel frames. It was a way to practice painting different textures and reflective surfaces without getting too hung up on the context.

I assumed this painting, with my fledgling ability and idiosyncratic content, would have no commercial potential, so I was pleasantly surprised when it sold to an artist and collector before the paint was dry. After she took it home she noticed I hadn't signed it and asked if I'd make a trip to her house on Bainbridge Island to do so. When I arrived, she gave me a thick pen with a kind of acrylic paint in it that I'd never used before. I pressed the retractable nib to the canvas and a splotch of white paint spurted onto the canvas near the tulips. Fortunately, a quick wipe with a paper towel saved it.

A Day In The Life, 2008
Oil 48" x 36"
(Opposite)

A Day In The Life (Sketchbook Notes), 2008
Uni-Ball pen, 11" x 8.5"

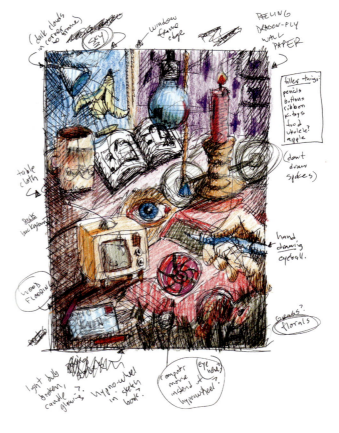

A Day In The Life (Plan), 2008
Uni-Ball pen and Prismacolor pencil, 11" x 8.5"

I made some notes for a large painting during a morning ferry ride. For the trip home, I forgot my Uni-Ball pen so I used the red Bic I carried with me for grading student papers. I had no references so the proportions were a little strange.

In Todd Schorr's book, **Secret Mystic Rites**, he includes a very brief section that shows step-by-step how he proceeds from a monochrome underpainting, or *grisaille*. The color is glazed over that in thin layers so the grisaille modeling shows through. I didn't know his method was the classic technique of the old masters, and still the way most figurative painters work. Maybe I was absent the day they taught that. I tried it with this painting. The refracted trees through the saltshaker and the reflections in the spoon are complete guesses. I've adopted the method for my watercolor paintings.

Edifice (Notes), 2009
Uni-Ball pen, 4" x 3"

Edifice (Plan), 2009
Uni-Ball pen, 4" x 3"

Edifice (Thumbnail), 2009
Ballpoint pen, 5" x 4"

Edifice (Grisaille), 2009
Oil, 48" x 36"

Edifice, 2009
Oil, 48" x 36"

Oil Painting

Open House, 2008
Oil, 36" x 24"

Trellis, 2009
Oil, 48" x 36"

Oil Painting

Bee, 2009
Oil, 36" x 30"

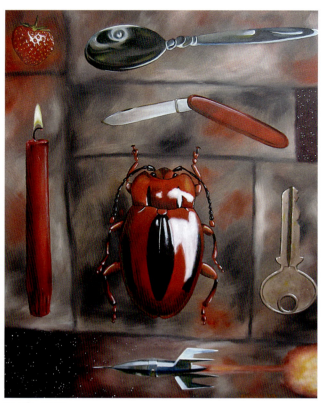

Beetle, 2009
Oil, 36" x 30"

Octopus, 2009
Oil, 48" x 36"
(Opposite)

I donated **Bee** (above, left) to the Gage Academy for its annual fund-raiser. Pamela Belyea, then the School's Director, hung the painting near her desk and forgot to put it in the auction. When she retired years later, she cleaned out her office and remembered that the painting was intended to be sold so she put it in the next auction. One morning, I was sitting in a Steering Committee meeting for Lawton Elementary School where I worked. A parent representative on the team asked me, "Do you paint?"

"Occasionally," I answered. "Why?"

"I think we own a painting of yours," he said.

Beetle (above, right), like all the paintings in the "rebus" style, was done with no intentional meaning outside the visual properties of the objects, yet more than one person has asked if this is a painting about drug use. I guess the knife, spoon, and flame create some kind of a drug allusion, but it wasn't my intent. It wouldn't be the first time I inadvertently conjured the demons of substance abuse (see **KP Lab**, page 185). I don't do drugs because I'm a bit of a control freak, I guess. I don't drink beer or wine and my mochas are decaffeinated. I don't smoke, either. My body is a temple. A temple made of chocolate.

*I submitted **Octopus** (opposite) into the Gage Alumni Show and forgot about it. Weeks later, I was on a first date near the school, and we went to look at the show. We couldn't find my painting. I thought they must have decided not to show it, or it was just too idiosyncratic for a school with a focus on classical figure studies. On the way out we stopped to look at the paintings in the Juried Competition, selected by the curator of the Seattle Art Museum. I was surprised to see I'd won in the Still-life category. I didn't know I'd even been considered for the contest. My prizes, a pile of art supplies and gift certificates, were still sitting in the room where the awards ceremony had been held. Not a bad turn of events for a first date.*

Portrait of Shannon, 2009
Oil, 36" x 36"

I first met Shannon at the Century Ballroom. She had recently moved to Seattle. Her Texas Two-Step clashed awkwardly with my East Coast Swing, but she was cool—smart, candid, and funny—and we became fast friends.

I asked her to put together a dozen things for me to paint, and she handed me a shoe-box of items which I arranged into a *Portrait of Shannon* (above). The objects are things she's collected that hold personal significance for her: a photo of her mother, a whisk from her boyfriend, a donkey-shaped bottle-opener that was her father's.

My stepmother then asked me to paint a "portrait" of my father. I approached *Larry* (opposite) the same way as *Shannon*, but I had to use reference photos since he lives in Sidney, Iowa.

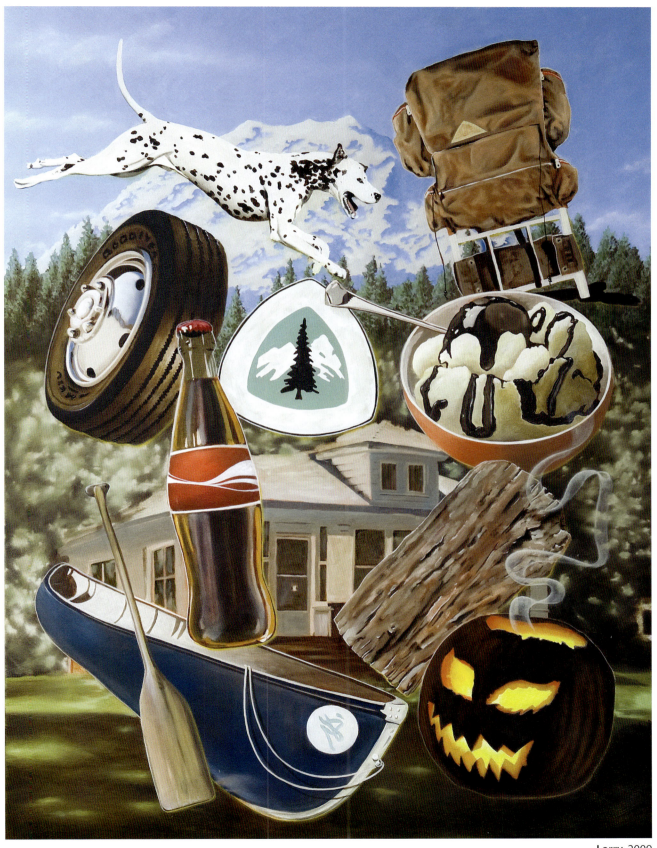

Larry, 2009
Oil, 48" x 36"

Oil Painting 239

SIDNEY

He reads every book in his home but it is not enough. The country boy craves stories. He devours every poem and fable in his school and library. Still he hungers. For stories.

-Jennifer Lanthier, **The Stamp Collector**

My great-grandparents were born in Sidney, a shrinking little farm town of 1200 people on the western edge of Iowa, near Omaha, where I was born. Great-grandma Lucretia lived to be 100 and her kids, Ruthella and Robert, are 93 and 95 and live there still. If pre-existing conditions count against you when applying for health insurance, I should get credit for the longevity of my kinfolk.

When Great-grandma Lucretia died, Grandma Ruthella inherited her house, but she already had one so she sold it to my dad. He still lives in it with my step-mom, Diane. It's in the painting on page 239. (Mt. Rainier is in the background because my dad loves to hike there.) I stayed with them for a month when I returned from China. Though I enjoyed the peace and quiet, I would go stir-crazy, like Jack Torrence in *The Shining*, after being too long with no cultural life or access to the arts.

I asked my dad to say something about the appeal of small town life:

"People know and care about each other," he said. "Today I got some mail the Postal Service wouldn't forward. We're friendly with the post master, so even though the mail had a different name, she put it in an envelope with a nice personal note. The phone guy gave me wire and information so I could do my own installation. When I asked to borrow a neighbor's lawn aerator, he delivered it to the house. I repaired it, inflated the tires and returned it. It's just the way people in the town are. The high school band practices marching in the streets around the school. We don't lock doors unless we're going to be away for long periods. My mom gets "meals-on-wheels" Monday through Friday and if my mom's not home, the volunteers put it in the refrigerator for her. I guess that's why we're here."

Sidney House, 2012
Watercolor, 9" x 12"

Downtown Sidney, 2012
Ink wash, 9" x 12"

Sidney Barn, 2012
Ink wash, 9" x 12"

Sidney Pipes, 2012
India ink, 11" x 8.5"

Draper House, 2012
Watercolor, 10" x 8"

Dead Bird, 2012
Watercolor, 6" x 8"

Above my father's front yard, this bird could be seen hanging below its nest. It was too high to figure out what had happened. I thought by drawing it I could sort it out. Could I see a fishing line? Was the bird entangled and strangled? Was it hooked on that stick behind its head? We couldn't figure it out.

Everyone in Sidney refers to this place (above) as "The Draper House" for the widow who lived there for decades. As I sat in the front yard drawing it, Danny, the new owner, a young shirtless guy with long hair in a pony tail, was laying paving stones at the foot of the front stairway. I showed him the finished drawing, and he gave me a tour. He had recently moved here with his wife because they could buy this huge house for only 50K. It's an interesting maze-like building with a lot of character and unique architectural features. Danny's wife planned to turn the upstairs into a yoga studio.

Their young son was an artist. We went upstairs to his huge room so he could show me his video-game and skateboarder-inspired drawings. On the wall was a poster of the rapper Tupac, which struck me as funny in this sleepy, little-town setting.

As we talked, a weird kind of symmetry emerged: Danny had a brother named Steve who had recently passed away in his twenties. My name is Steve, and I had a brother named Danny who also died in his twenties.

TEACHING

Over the last forty years, many educators, decision-makers, and even some parents have come to regard the arts as peripheral, and let's face it, frivolous—especially the visual arts, with their connotation of "the starving artist" and the mistaken concept of "necessary talent."

-Betty Edwards

It's not natural to sit as often as we do, yet there are so many times when we are expected to. Trapped, we bounce our heel against the floor, twirl our hair, bite our fingernails. I hear they give *Jeopardy* contestants paper-clips to bend and twist so they have something to do with their non-buzzer hands when they have to wait through commercial breaks and other down times. Someday sitting will be all that's left me. Until then, I sit as little as possible. I teach on my feet. I go for walks at lunch. During staff meetings I often stand in the back of the room and draw.

It's especially cruel to expect children to sit still, yet that's what we keep telling them. "Sit down. Hold still. Listen. Stop that." All day long, during assemblies, lined up for lunch or recess, school bus rides, listening to their peers give oral reports. They don't have ADD or ADHD. They're *kids*.

But they have to sit at their desks most of the time, of course, or chaos would reign. I let my students draw while I read aloud or any time they finish their work early. They are perfectly capable of listening to me read aloud while doodling at the same time. In most cases, it helps focus their concentration and retention. Sometimes, even without my prompting them, they illustrate the scenes or characters in the stories I read. If I don't let them draw, they secretly break up erasers into little crumbs or scratch things on the desk with their safety scissors.

Meet The New Boss, 2011
Ink wash, 8.5" x 11"

Staff Meeting, 2010
Ink wash, 8.5" x 11"

My colleagues are dedicated professionals who come early and stay late. They spend weekends in the classroom tailoring lessons to suit specific kids with special needs. We rub each other the wrong way sometimes because we're passionate about how we believe things should be. Many of us are friends outside of school. We go out, shoot pool, or play volleyball on Friday nights. I attend their weddings, and they come to my art shows. Good people.

My Staff Meeting Notes, 2010
Ink, 8.5" x 11"

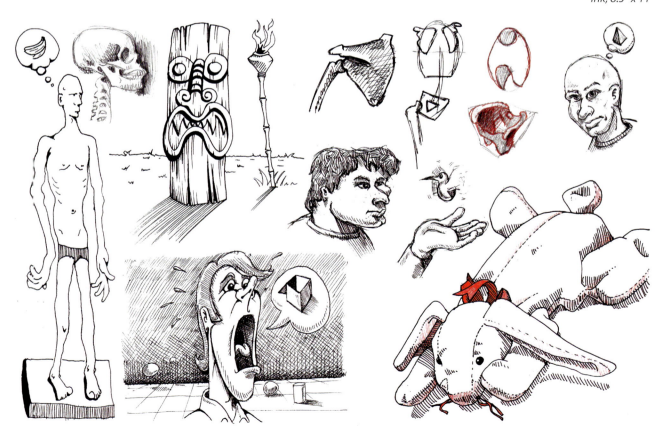

Teaching 245

Another Staff Meeting, 2009
Ink wash, 8.5" x 11"

More Meeting Notes, 2009
Ink, 8.5" x 11"

Professional Development, 2009
Ink wash, 8.5" x 11"

Another Meeting, 2012
Watercolor, 3.5" x 11"

More Meeting Notes Again, 2009
Uni-ball pen, 6" x 8"

Teaching 247

Guest Author, 2012
Ink wash 3.5" x 11"

When I'm with the kids, my previous life of eclectic, unfocused flitting from one passion to another pays off. I enjoy reading aloud, prompting student writing, preparing skits, making art, performing music, and recreating historic events—all of it. Kids are interested in everything. A discussion of plate tectonics and volcanoes could arise from a student's trip to Hawaii and evolve into a tangent on state's rights or air pollution or the relativity of "up" and "down" on a globe. It's fun to follow digressions wherever their enthusiasm leads. My students keep me young. They teach me about the games, books and music they're into, and their families have me to dinner and come watch me perform in plays or buy my prints at art openings.

Sadly, the competition for federal funding limits the ability of teachers to tailor lessons to specific demographics. With the increasing emphasis on test results, I'm asked to simplify. Focus on the data. Raise those test scores. Spend less time creating plays and more time preparing for tests that the kids take in the computer lab. Let the music teacher handle the concerts. Parent volunteers teach art for half an hour a month so teachers will concentrate on test prep. My integrated history/science/reading/writing/art unit on Thor Heyerdahl's voyage on the *Kon-Tiki*? *No time*, I'm told. Civics? *Not on the test.* The curriculum and delivery methods are streamlined, one-size-fits all—all teachers, all kids.

This is silly. The factory model of education—that kids are products on an assembly line that must meet specific standards—is an outdated paradigm that ignores individual strengths and differences and—

Sorry. I get a little worked up about this. Now where was I?

Kids, 2012
Watercolor, 7" x 10"

Teaching is Humbling, 2013
Watercolor, 11" x 8.5"

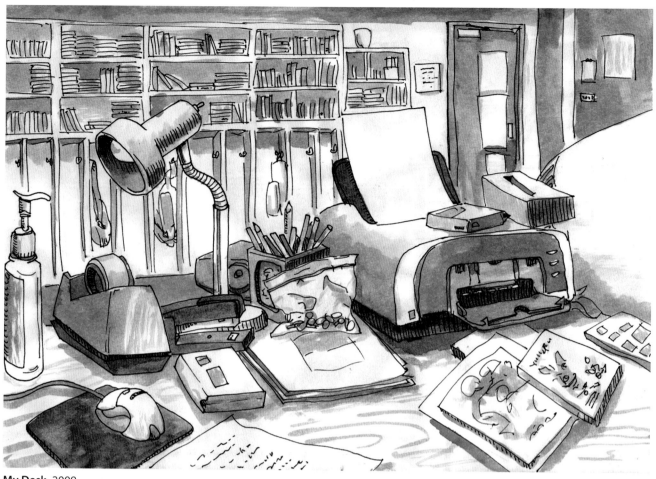

My Desk, 2009
Ink wash, 8.5" x 11"

School Assembly, 2013
Ink wash, 8.5" x 11"

Simon, 2013
Watercolor, 14" x 11"
(Opposite)

Simon's mom asked me to draw something for his birthday. Simon is a funny and bright kid who loves math. He's a well-rounded student with great parents. His mom Laura put together an adult drawing class for me to teach. Each week the class was hosted in a different house in Seattle's upscale Magnolia neighborhood. Ten ladies drinking wine, telling stories and drawing from themed still-lifes. A dream job!

A Teacher's Nightmare

Teacher's Nightmare, 2013
Watercolor, 11" x 17"

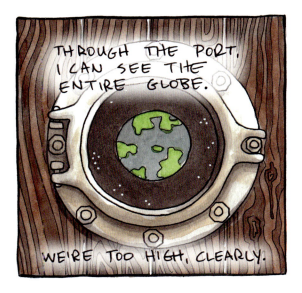

HOME IS WHERE THE ART IS

The only work really worth doing—the only work you can do convincingly—is the work that focuses on the things you care about. Your job is to draw a line from your life to your art that is straight and clear.

-David Bayles and Ted Orland, **Art and Fear**

Adventure!, 1981
Ball Point Pen, 11" x 17"

A diary entry from Berkeley, California, with my high school girlfriend. I was 19.

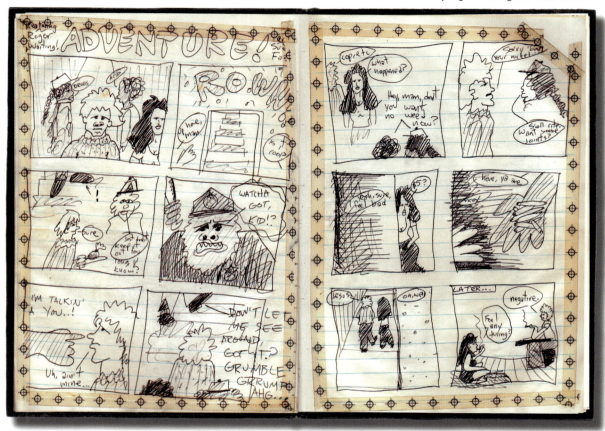

I vacillate between drawing safe, objective things—houses, vintage shops, piles of clutter—and more personal drawings about relationships or states of mind. The former are much easier, of course; see a house, draw a house. Personal pieces are more challenging, not technically, but in the psychic energy needed to tweak them, to make them presentable. When I look through my sketchbooks and think about my next book, it's the personal pieces, the diary-style narrative drawings, flawed as they are, that still speak to me.

I want to draw the way Montaigne wrote his journals—impetuously and uncensored, but I don't want to embarrass myself. How do I draw my frustration with the dental issues I'm having? How do I depict the perpetual struggle between autonomy and loneliness?

Sequential illustrations (comics) are well-suited for telling personal stories. The spandex-clad super-heroes and over-simplified stories of good and evil in traditional comic books seemed to me, even as a kid, repetitive and irrelevant as Big Time Wrestling. But the artists in *Heavy Metal* explored thought-provoking stories about subjective perception and ethical dilemmas. The magazine has long ceased being the showcase for talented narrative artists such as Enki Bilal, Philippe Caza, Philippe Druillet, and Moebius. But mature and autobiographical themes are being explored by many serious "cartoonists." Works such as **Maus** by Art Speigelman, which won the 1992 Pulitzer Prize, or Robert Crumb's illustrated biography of **Kafka** and his literal rendering of the entire book of **Genesis**, are a long way from the teenage pratfalls of the Archies or the thinly-disguised homo-erotica of Batman and Robin.

HOUSEBOUND

Housebound, 2013
Ink wash, 14" x 11"

For many years I rarely got sick. If I did miss work, I used personal days to be with my son. But after returning from Asia, and being re-assigned to the younger second-graders, I was sick with sinus infections for much of a year.

Home Is Where The Art Is

Discovery Park Run

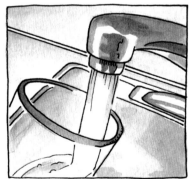

Discovery Park Run, 2013
Ink wash, 14" x 20"

June 7, 2013, one week before I quit my job, I have this dream.

It's early evening. I'm walking with a friend as shops are closing. Through a lowering security gate, I recognize George Clooney.

"George!" I say, "Gary Faigin* and I are moving the Wednesday night figure drawing sessions to Fremont. I hope you'll come."

He finishes paying and ducks under the gate. "I see you have your sketchbook with you," I say. "Mind if I take a look?"

He's reluctant but too polite to say no.

*Founder and Art Director of GAGE Academy.

His sketches remind me of Mattias Adolfsson's work. As I flip through the pages, it begins to rain.

Unwilling to let this end, I lead him off the sidewalk to a nearby brownstone.

"You'll be dry under these eaves," I say. "Wait here a second."

I climb a few steps for a better angle.

I tell him I'll protect his book with my body.

Just above George's head, part of the downspout is missing or broken.

I Dream of Clooney, 2013
Watercolor, 11" x 16"

Home Is Where The Art Is

Movie Review, 2013
Ink wash, 10" x 8"

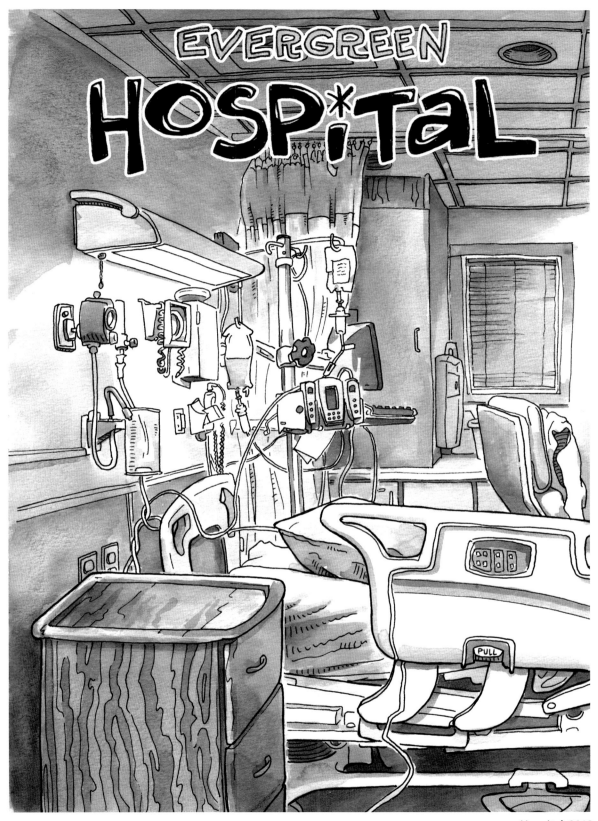

Hospital, 2012
Ink wash, 12" x 9"

Grandma Ruthella fell and cracked her pelvis. I drew while she ate lunch. We watched Cash Cab with the subtitles on because her hearing aid was on the fritz. Otherwise, she was in fine fettle.

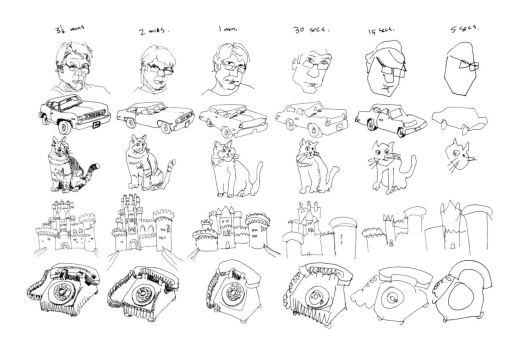

Speed Exercise, 2013
India ink, 14" x 18"

*Ivan Brunetti is a prolific and talented cartoonist whose work often appears on the cover of **The New Yorker**, among other places. I first became aware of him when he edited **An Anthology of Graphic Fiction, Cartoons, & True Stories** (Yale University Press, 2006).*

*The exercises on these pages are from his book, **Cartooning: Philosophy and Practice** (Yale University Press, 2011), a workbook for people like me who want to improve their graphic storytelling ability.*

Brunetti Lesson, 2013
Ink wash, 9" x 12"

Stop-Time, 2013
Watercolor, 5" x 6"

Exercise 2.4 in Brunetti's workbook on cartooning is to try to capture the mood of an entire book in one panel. I chose Frank Conroy's excellent memoir **Stop-Time**. Conroy tells about his poor childhood, growing up with his mom and step-dad. I appreciate how Conroy is candid and poignant, without being whiny and maudlin.

Bright Lights, 2013
Ink wash, 5" x 6"

Exercise 2.4b is similar to the previous one but with an emphasis on simplification. I chose the scene in McInerney's **Bright Lights, Big City** where "your" younger brother Michael forces the climactic confrontation. (The book is told in second-person present tense, as if you are the main character.) Reliving the memory of your mother's final days allows you to begin dealing with the suppressed feelings that have lead you to a life of excess and drug abuse.

High Fidelity, 2013
Ink wash, 5" x 6"

I appreciate Brunetti's emphasis on "not trying to be funny." In spite of the name, there's nothing inherent in "comics" that requires them to be "comical." Lesson 2.4c requires more simplification. No color. Clean lines. Readability. This is the scene after the funeral where Rob hides from his estranged girlfriend to avoid admitting he's sorry.

Brunetti Lesson 2.1, 2013
Ink wash, 10" x 15"

Christmas, 2012
Ink wash, 10" x 8"

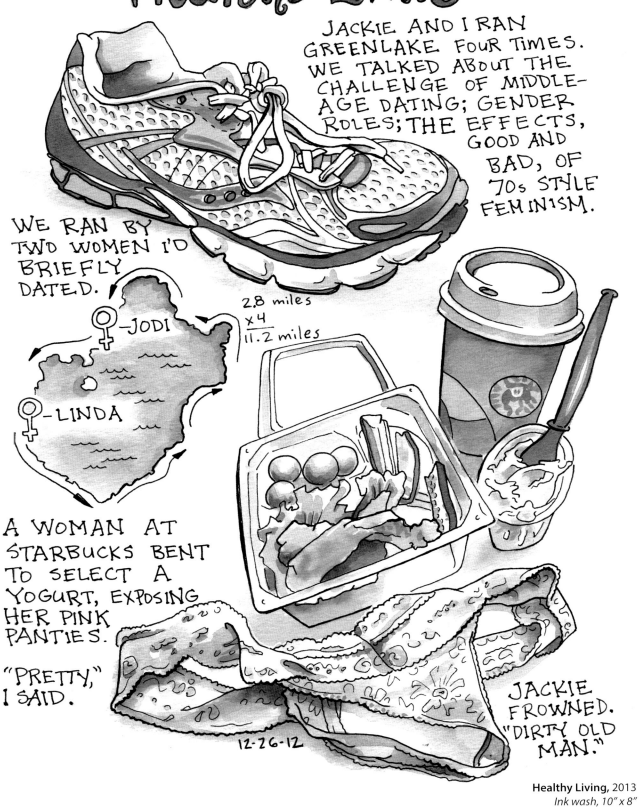

Healthy Living, 2013
Ink wash, 10" x 8"

I Am What I Eat, 2012
Ink wash, 10" x 8"

Morning Errands, 2012
Ink wash, 10" x 8"

Sub Driver, 2012
Ink wash 10" x 8"

Bad Mocha, 2013
Ink wash 10" x 8"

The News, 2013
Ink wash, 10" x 14"

Lipstick, 1991
Prismacolor, 11" x 8.5"

Puzzle, 1991
Prismacolor, 11" x 8.5"

Catharsis, 1991
India ink, 8" x 11"

Home Is Where The Art Is

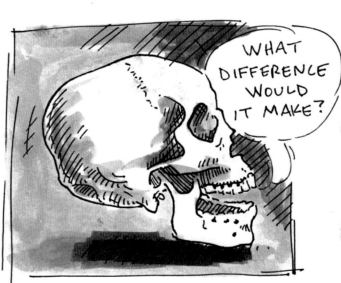

3 Practical Questions, 2009
Ink wash, 10" x 8"

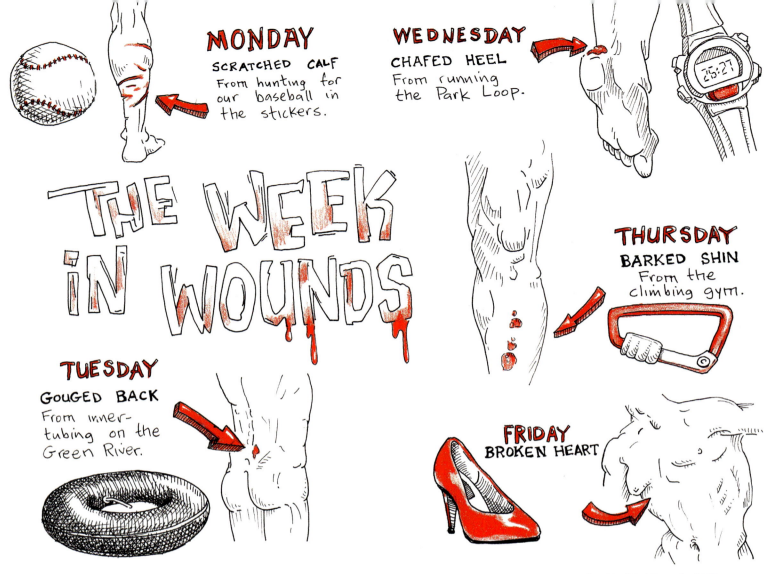

The Week In Wounds, 2008
Uni-ball and Prismacolor, 10" x 16"

Dana, the guy who shared his journal with me in high school, inspiring my obsession with sketch-booking, was a charismatic artist and actor. He played the lead in our high-school production of *The Music Man*. He also designed the sets and created the poster. After he left for college, I spent the summer learning the lead role for my senior-year production of *Carousel*. I got the part. Emulating Dana, I designed the sets and created the posters, as well. When Dana came home for winter break, he offered to help me with the designs. I felt defensive. I didn't want help. For years I'd been a stranger in each new school, and now I was recognized through theater, from art, from music. I told him no.

"I thought we were friends," he said.

"You had your turn," I explained. "This is mine." He had once written in his journal *Steve's a good guy*, but now he looked at me and said, "You're an asshole."

After the show closed, another friend was over while I worked in my journal, drawing a comic. I'd just made the "talk bubble" for a very poorly-drawn woman. Laughing at my drawing, I asked my friend to come take a look.

"What should I have her say?"

My friend looked surprised. "What do you mean?" he asked.

"What do I put in the balloon here? I mean what should she be saying?"

"I can't tell you that," he said.

"Why not?"

"Because that's the whole idea behind you. You always have to do everything by yourself."

He went back to flipping through my record LPs as I drew. After a while he said, "I've always depended on the kindness of strangers."

I turned to him. "What?"

"That's what she should say: 'I've always depended on the kindness of strangers.'"

As a little kid, short of breath and unable to gain weight, my little brother was diagnosed with Pulminary Veno-Occlusive Disease, a rare lung disorder with no cure. Still, Dan could do a standing back flip from the ground and land on his feet. He was an avid and frequent skydiver. He played piano. He moved to Hollywood and got bit parts in movies that played up his skinny frame and unusual features. Embracing his lank physique, he entered a Mr. Puni-verse competition and brought home the first place trophy. He told me when he dropped his robe for the poses, the other contestants threw in the towel, literally.

Dan took me to a poker game with some guys he barely knew. The first one out of chips, I played video games while Dan took everyone's money. The last guy, however, would not let it end. He challenged Dan to shorter and shorter games, losing more and more money. Finally, angry and desperate to get his money back, he insisted that Dan cut the cards—high card takes all. Dan whispered to me to go start the car and wait for him. In minutes he came running out the door and dove through the passenger window with the guys yelling and running after him. Still breathing hard, he handed me $50—my poker game buy-in.

We were college roommates, business partners, and friends. When he finally got paged from the University of Washington, he was eager for his lung transplant because he was going to pursue a career in tennis. But the lung, from an athlete in Alaska, was too big. His worn out little chest rejected it and Dan died after a grueling year-long fight to stay alive with his one remaining defective lung. He was 29.

I Dream of Dan, 1991
Ink, 11" x 8"

My son was born four months after my brother died, and because they have a lot in common, there's a strange sort of continuity for me. Kalen picks up where Dan left off. In my dreams and memories, I often confuse them. Sharing an anecdote I'll say, "Yesterday, my son, no, my brother said he was, no, my son said... ."

Kalen and Dan are/were both "guy's guys," meaning they have/had lots of male friends, whereas I put all my eggs in the basket of a girlfriend. Kalen and Dan are/were athletes, excelling at whatever sport or activity they attempt. I was bookish and spent my time indoors reading, drawing or learning an instrument. They are/were charming. I can be opinionated and critical. Everyone loves/loved Kalen and Dan. Great guys, both of them. Although I'm the dad/older brother, I try to learn from their examples.

Warp-Speed, 1991
Ink, 24" x 18"

9 Mile Waterfront Run

Warefront Run, 2013
Ink wash, 11" x 17"

11 Self-portraits, 2013
Ink wash, 9" x 11"

Dan Clowes, Charles Burns, Chris Ware, Peter Bagge, Roz Chast, Jim Flora, Seth, Mitch O'Connell, Ben Katchor, KAZ, Marc Bell

11 More Self-portraits, 2013
Ink wash, 9" x 11"

Joe Sacco, Julie Doucet, Joost Swarte, Kim Dietch, Robert Crumb, Jim Woodring, Joe Matt, Derek Yaniger, Chris Garbutt, Joe Coleman, Dave Cooper

A Walk in the Park

WHEN THINGS ARE GOOD

WHEN I GO TO BED EARLY,

RESIST THE URGE TO STAY UP LATE

TO GET MORE ACCOMPLISHED,

I FEEL EERILY WEIGHTLESS—

A Walk in the Park, 2013
Watercolor, 11" x 16"

Robin's Home, 2013
Watercolor, 9" x 12"

Robin Fuchs, an artist and photographer, sat on the grass beside me as I drew her beautiful house in Hanover, Maryland. We talked about art and the influence that Danny Gregory and Gabriel Campanario have had on us. Robin's young daughter Emmy drew a picture of herself and gave it to me to bring home to Seattle.

CROWDSOURCING

Artists come together with the clear knowledge that when all is said and done, they will return to their studio and practice art alone. Period. That simple truth may be the deepest bond we share.

-David Bayles, **Art and Fear**

Though this book wants to be about independence and autonomy, there are many people to whom it owes a huge debt of gratitude. Their friendship, support, and enthusiasm for the drawings was a lifeline as I lay awake at 3 a.m. full of doubts, questioning the value of what I do.

I first learned about crowdsourcing from my cousins, Emily and Mollie. They perform vintage, Americana music duets as *Douglas County Daughters*. I contributed to their Kickstarter campaign to help pay for the studio time and production of their latest CD, *Going Home*. Just as I began to think about a campaign to fund *Now Where Was I?*, I was contacted by videographer Deborah Libby. I knew Deborah from our classes in TESOL, Teaching English to Speakers of Other Languages. She wanted to shoot a documentary about my process. I'm sure I owe much of the success of my own Kickstarter campaign to her excellent little film.

Special thanks also to the supporters whose homes I've included here.

Brad's House, 2013
Watercolor, 12" x 9"

Brad Mohr's home is very near my apartment in the Ravenna neighborhood of North Seattle.

Seahawks, 2013
Watercolor, 9" x 12"

Roy Forbes lives in Japan. When I asked how I could show my appreciation for his generous support, he said he missed Seattle and suggested I draw something Seahawks-related.

The Plonskis', 2013
Watercolor, 9" x 12"

This is the view from the Plonskis' "back-40" in Connecticut, where we sat around the bonfire and ate pit-roasted potatoes, corn, and hamburgers until I was so full I fell asleep in my lawn chair.

Christine Legere's, 2013
Watercolor, 9" x 12"

Rich's Art, 2013
Watercolor, 9" x 12"

Rich Goodnight sees a piece of art he likes, in any medium, and says, "I can do that." Then he teaches himself how to do it. He works in leather, ink, paint, watercolor, wood, folded paper, you name it. A real Renaissance Man, even his home in Valparaiso, Indiana is a work of art.

I've given up my secure position with Seattle Public Schools to draw full-time. It wasn't the "smart" thing to do, at least not fiscally. I had great health coverage, I had a strong union that fought on my behalf, I was contributing 15% of my salary to a 401K. I was proud of being a teacher.

Now I have no steady income. No sooner had my insurance run out than I learned I needed two root canals. Two poorly-made crowns needed replacing. And last week I got a $200 speeding ticket for going 27 mph in a school zone. I'll probably never be able to retire.

On the other hand, I was hired to teach several drawing workshops at the Gage Academy. I'm being commissioned to make drawings. I teach art classes to adults. My previous dentist refunded the money I paid for the original sloppy crowns so I could have them redone properly by my new dentist.

And I talked the judge into cutting my speeding fine in half.

As for retiring, why would I want to retire from doing what I love? Retire to do what? All I've ever really wanted was mobility, options and time. Check, check and check. And I have the next book project already underway.

Donna is a marriage and family therapist. She's terrific. I think she gets me. I'm going to try hard not to mess this up.

Workshop Demos, 2013
Watercolor, 8" x 11" each

Donna at Work, 2013
Watercolor, 9" x 12"

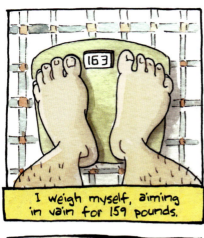

Index

A

Acapulco 47, 221–222, 225, 227
Adler, Charles 77, 80
Americus, Georgia 119
Anchorage, Alaska 47, 170, 176, 216
Anderson, Darold 75
An Illustrated Journey (Gregory) 120
An Illustrated Life (Gregory) 120
Atlanta, Georgia 119
Atlas Vintage Mall 57, 62, 63, 64, 65, 67, 68, 69

B

Baijiu 120
Bainbridge Island, Washington 230
Baker, Nicholson 164
Baker, Rick 216
Ballard Neighborhood, Seattle 44, 138, 152
Bangkok, Thailand 47, 160, 162
Batcave, The 81
Belltown Neighborhood, Seattle 152
Boca Raton, Florida 188
Bremerton, Washington 55, 228
Bright Lights, Big City (McInerney) 263
Broward County, Florida 30
Brunetti, Ivan 262–265
Bruno, Dave 86
Buckner, Paul 168
Bukowski, Charles 170
Burbank, California 81
Burke-Gilman Trail 44

C

California College of the Arts 254
Campanario, Gabriel 9, 133, 151, 284
card game(s)
    52 Card Pick-Up 13
    Dou Dizhu (Fight the Landlord) 121
    Pinochle 34, 39
    poker 22, 276
Carlin, George 13
cartoon (defined) 107
Cascade Mountains 44
Chao Phraya River 160
China 47, 83, 95, 97–131
Chinatown (Vancouver B.C.) 139
Chittenden Locks 44
Christmas 128
Clooney, George 259
Club Street, Singapore 189
Communist Party 107, 108
Conroy, Frank 263
Cortez, Sea of 22
Crumb, Robert 254
Curb Your Enthusiasm 130

D

Davenport, Joy 182
Degas, Edgar 228
Deluxe Junk 65
Dimond High School, Anchorage 176
Discovery Park, Seattle 33, 147, 256
divorce 13, 32
Drawing Jam 134, 186, 187

E

El Golfo, Mexico 22
Emerald Downs 34, 39
Episodes 81
Eugene, Oregon 216
Everyday Matters (Gregory) 120
Experience Music Project 135

F

Fisherman's Terminal 62, 155
Flickr 133
Florida State University 31
Fort Collins, Colorado 47
Four Seasons Hotel 139
Fred Flintstone 108, 193
Fremont Coffee Company 53
Fremont Neighborhood, Seattle 53, 67
Frisell, Bill 41

G

Gage Academy 134–135, 164–168, 186–187, 229, 236, 289
Gao Ling 98, 105, 110, 117–130
Gasworks Park 42–43, 46, 53
Georgetown Neighborhood, Seattle 148, 157
Graduate, The 37
Greenlake Neighborhood, Seattle 20
Green River 34, 44, 229
Gregory, Danny 9, 120, 136, 284
grisaille 107, 232

H

Halloween 108, 216
Hatchet (Paulson) 29
Hawaii 47
Heavy Metal Magazine 254
Helfgott, Jackie 9, 65, 138, 139, 143, 144, 145, 267
Hendrix, Jimi 41, 54
Heyerdahl, Thor 86, 248
High Fidelity (Hornby) 263
Hollywood, California 77, 138, 276
Hutian Kiln, China 97

I

Ingeborg 123
Irish (family) 94

J

Jack Block Park, Seattle 135
Jiffy Lube 110, 140
Jingdezhen Ceramic Institute 98
Jingdezhen, China 47
Jingdezhen Pottery Studio 103
Jiujiang, China 110
Joshua Tree Park, California 77, 80

K

Kane, Tommy 136
Kerouac, Jack 170
Kickstarter 9
Kodiak Island, Alaska 13, 47
Kon-Tiki 86, 248

L

Lake Union, Seattle 43, 46, 75, 141
Lake Washington Ship Canal 53
Lawton Elementary School, Seattle 142, 236, 248–257
Leng Shui Jian Mountain, China 119
Lenin, Vladimir 53
Leonard, Sarah 59–61
Long Beach, California 77–85, 83, 184
Los Angeles, California 81
Louis CK 130, 158

M

Magnolia Neighborhood, Seattle 18, 250
Mandarin 95, 110, 114, 119, 121, 124
Mao Zedong 113, 123
Men of a Certain Age 81
Mexico 22, 77
Micronesia 83
Mitchell, Joni 110
mocha(s) 39, 110, 230–231, 271
Monroe Prison, Washington State 151
Montaigne 193, 254
Mort's Cabin 75
Myrtle Edwards Park, Seattle 44

N

Nanhe River, China 114
Nicholson, Jack 240
Nova Scotia 47
Nye, Bill 41

O

Oakland, California 254
oil painting 90–91, 228–239
Olympic Mountains 44
Omaha, Nebraska 13

P

Pacific Galleries 73
Paulson, Gary 29
Peace Corps 83, 95
people (drawing) 164–187
Pioneer Square Neighborhood, Seattle 50
Playa Bonfil, Mexico 221
Pottery Workshop, The 111, 123
Preszler, Cyrena 59–61
Puget Sound, Washington 44, 48, 55
Puyallup, Washington 13

Q

Quiksilver 77

R

Ravenna Neighborhood, Washington 285
Ravensdale, Washington 34
Reddy, Dan 216, 230, 243, 276, 277
Reddy, Kalen 30-39, 276
Robinson Crusoe (Defoe) 86
roller derby 108, 179

S

San Bao, China 99, 114, 127
San Francisco, California 47, 170
San Juan Capistrano, California 77, 81
Savini, Tom 216
Seattle Art Museum 236
Seattle Pacific University 30
Seattle School District 73
Seattle University 51
Seattle, Washington 30, 34, 41, 57, 94, 250
Seeking A Friend For The End of the World 260
Shanghai, China 97
Shilshole Marina, Seattle 156
Shining, The (King) 240
Sidney, Iowa 238–243
Silhouette 57
Singapore 47, 191
Skagit River 47
Slovakia 53
South Beach, Florida 47
Southern California 83
South Pacific 95, 182
Speigelman, Art 254
Stop-Time (Conroy) 263
Suzallo Library (University of Washington)) 150
Swenson, Ric 98, 176
Swiss Family Robinson (Wyss) 86

T

Tacoma, Washington 13
TESOL (Teaching English to Speakers of Other Languages) 13, 48, 95
Thailand 160
The 100 Thing Challenge (Bruno) 86
The Creative License (Gregory) 120
The Daily Show 130
Tia Boon Sim 191
tiki(s) 54, 55, 91, 94, 182, 230–231, 248
Trove Vintage Boutique 57, 59

U

University of Oregon 13, 168, 170
Urban Sketcher(s) 133–158

V

Valparaiso, Indiana 287
Vancouver B.C. 139

W

Wang, Johanna 110
Washington State 13, 41
Wat Phra Kaew 160
West Virginian Exchange Students 108
Wong, Gail 134
Woodring, Jim 10, 41

Y

Yuen Ren Chao 124
Yuma, Arizona 22

Coffee Shop, 2012
Ink wash, 8" x 11"

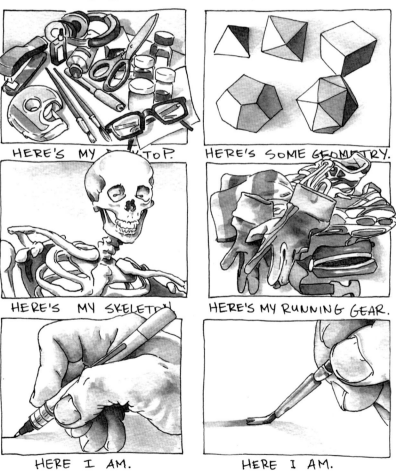